Equity-Based Leadership

Equity-Based Leadership

Leveraging Complexity
to Transform School Systems

Joshua P. Starr

HARVARD EDUCATION PRESS
CAMBRIDGE, MA

Paperback ISBN 978-1-68253-728-2

Library of Congress Cataloging-in-Publication Data is on file.

Published by Harvard Education Press,
an imprint of the Harvard Education Publishing Group

Harvard Education Press
8 Story Street
Cambridge, MA 02138

Cover Design: Ciano Design

The typefaces in this book are Minion Pro.

Contents

INTRODUCTION

Context Matters

WITHIN ALMOST 14,000 school districts in America there are approximately 3.7 million teachers, millions of support professionals, hundreds of thousands of building leaders, and thousands of central office leaders, all guided by the work of a superintendent and school board. Every day educators come to work within the context of their communities and districts, intending to teach and support students. The measure of their efforts is in the state accountability system, which typically considers annual state standardized test scores, graduation rates, attendance, and sometimes other local factors such as school climate data, arts participation, and community service. Educators spend all of their time trying to move the needle on these metrics: increase the graduation rate, increase the percentage of students from different backgrounds who pass the math portion of the state test, ensure young people are coming to school ready to learn, and provide additional services and supports when necessary. Rinse and repeat. Federal, state, and local funds are allocated to provide more interventions, services, and programs to students who are falling behind. Additional periods are scheduled to give more support, social workers and reading specialists are hired to intervene, new curriculum and technologies are purchased with the promise that they hold the key to improving student achievement.

Yet despite all of this effort and promises of change, too many students aren't achieving standards, and educators are still looking for solutions. Throughout the nation, school district leaders, superintendents in particular, are working to implement new strategies grounded in equity and sometimes face resistance or simply don't succeed. Leaders need a new approach. This book provides system leaders a path to transforming their systems through an equity lens. By offering examples from my own experience and that of superintendents who have worked to align their districts around a coherent equity strategy, this book gives leaders a framework for transforming their systems. The six elements of transformation I describe are the entry points for that journey.

Teaching and learning is the place to begin a transformation effort, as what adults do every day with students in classrooms is the essence of schools. System leaders must then organize around shared *values*, be explicit and transparent about *decision-making*, *allocate resources* according to vision and need, and *manage people* to achieve new levels of performance. All of this happens within the system's *culture*. This book is intended to help superintendents and system leaders organize an equity-based transformation agenda by focusing on these six entry points.

I use the term *entry point* to suggest that there are no single solutions or one way of doing things. I also refer to *superintendents* and *system leaders* interchangeably while making distinctions when appropriate. As this book is based on my experience and that of others who have led or are currently leading school systems, the stories and examples are from that perspective. But district cabinet members play significant roles in system-wide transformation efforts and, as Honig and Rainey have shown us, are key players in driving improvement.[1]

While school districts typically look similar, each context is different, and every leader's story is their own. If there's no one-size-fits-all approach to school improvement, neither is their one for systems transformation. There are, however, some key principles that leaders should attend to as they enact a comprehensive transformation strategy. There are essential questions to ask about whether the system is optimally organized for equity and excellence. I use the term *entry point* to suggest that it is up to the leader to determine how they will engage in a process of organizing their teams, communities, and schools around a clear set of guiding principles upon which their transformation effort rests.

Much has been written about school improvement practices and effective schools. Most leaders learn change management theory, and there are countless books and articles about various policy, pedagogical, or technical solutions that promise significant change in how schools operate. Yet we don't tell enough stories about how real school system leaders drive a transformational equity agenda. I think we need to understand how leaders make difficult choices within the context of their complex systems if we hope to understand how to better organize our school districts so that they serve our children at a higher level. This book attempts to do just that.

I also think that rather than focus solely on student learning, we must also attend to the daily practice of adults within a coherent and aligned system. I use the term *system* throughout this book to describe the interconnected actions of adults and young people within a district and schools. Every day in school districts people are doing something that should be leading toward a larger goal. Those actions may be distinctly connected to each other, or they may be intentionally or unintentionally discrete. I believe that the job of a leader is to ensure that schools and central offices are working in concert around a shared set of equity goals with a clear understanding of the practices that will lead to increased student achievement. For most of this century, too much of the discourse about public school improvement has been enamored with the promise of bold, sweeping changes devoid of context and appreciation for the actual change process itself. I believe we need to focus instead on the steady improvement of average adult practice. The policies, regulations, past practices, contractual agreements, and guidelines by which adults work within school systems make up the rules that guide short, near, and long-term actions. Those rules are complex. Leaders who hope to improve teaching and learning and increase student achievement need to embrace that complexity and rewrite the rules.

School system leaders today are also faced with an equity imperative. Our schools are more diverse than ever, and too many of our most vulnerable students aren't receiving the education they need to succeed in college and careers. Strides have been made in some schools and some districts by leaders who ensure that all students have access to high-quality instruction. Many educators have embraced the equity imperative by reallocating resources, providing necessary supports, regularly analyzing data, engaging the community, opening access to high-level courses, activating student voices, and ensuring that collaborative learning among adults is driving improvements in practice. These core elements of an equity agenda are hard to scale within a school district, and many leaders are just starting their equity journey and don't know where to begin. The six entry points I describe in this book are the starting points. The stories I tell of leaders provide examples of how to organize and drive an equity agenda.

Every school system exists within its own context, and every leader brings their own story to the work of transformation. System improvement will look different among various districts, even though there may be similar elements. Superintendents must adhere to certain core principles as they lead a transformation effort, but they must also do so authentically. A superintendent who's trying to transform their system through an equity lens has to organize their efforts around six entry points. An entry point can be a starting place for collective inquiry processes. Transformation starts with leaders identifying the problem they're trying to solve and then organizing processes that will lead to a change in adult practice intended to improve student achievement. School districts are incredibly complex systems that are judged by stakeholders based on their limited experiences in one part of it. A system leader's job is to see the gestalt. Yet they must enter into that whole in deliberate, intentional ways in order to lead others toward improvement. The six entry points in this book offer such an approach.

I also think it's important that superintendents and system leaders understand the history of school district design and how it influences and constrains them. We didn't get here by happenstance. Elected officials, the federal government, local school boards, and superintendents have made choices along the way about how they think school districts should be organized. Power and decision-making authority over personnel, curriculum, school construction, and resource allocation have been determined by statutes, policies, and contractual agreements that have emerged and calcified over time. While it's not reasonable to suggest a superintendent can change or disregard these long-standing strictures, I believe it's helpful to understand how they've come to be so that a leader can then know how to act differently. Santayana's maxim rings true: If we don't know our history, we're doomed to repeat it.

PURPOSE OF THIS BOOK

For more than twenty-five years I have been part of leading system-wide transformation efforts through an equity lens. In the late 1990s and early 2000s, as a cabinet member in a small urban district, I led the design of an accountability system that aligned our efforts to improve instruction, address social-emotional learning, and engage the community. In New York City I worked in the Joel Klein administration as that system was being radically overhauled, first on curriculum and programs and then on accountability system design. In my first superintendency I led an effort to detrack academic courses while raising standards and engaging the community. And in my second superintendency I began the process of shifting the rigid orientation of the system away from standardized tests and toward creative problem solving, social emotional learning, and higher academic standards. All of these efforts required a deep dive into the organization and alignment of the system itself. I learned how a leader can ensure that the interactions among people within a coherent framework grounded in equity and excellence are leading to the desired results. The six entry points I describe throughout this book provide leaders that framework.

I have also observed and learned from other leaders who are doing this difficult work and researchers who have studied what it takes to improve outcomes for young people. I wrote this book to try to capture what I've come to know as the overarching tenet of the superintendency: there is no single approach to change that will work in every context. Certainly, that's clear in the research and the lived experiences of anyone who has actually done the work in schools and systems. Yet, I've seen the marketplace, policy makers, and parents, sometimes amplified by the media, claim otherwise. Each leader must use their own experiences to navigate the complexity of the context they find themselves in. They need to build a great team, know the research, and build on and learn from the work of others. And there are principles that can be adhered to that I believe will lead to success. The six entry points and stories of leaders in this book will help system leaders begin an equity-based transformation effort.

In 1992, when I began substitute teaching in a NYC school for adolescents labeled with an intellectual disability, I had no idea it would lead to a career as an educator. I had always liked working with young people and knew that public service was my calling, but teaching wasn't on my radar. I needed a temporary job, though, before moving to the West Coast, and a good friend of the family was an Assistant Principal at the school and said I could easily get a substitute license. Ninety dollars a day was some real money, so I jumped at it. Once I got to San Francisco, there were few jobs available given the recession, but a group home for adolescents with mental health needs, many of whom were serving the last part of their sentences in the juvenile justice system, was hiring counselors. My eyes began to open to the gross inequities in the design of our public youth-serving systems.

When I returned to New York a year and a half later to take a teaching job in a school serving adolescents labeled with severe emotional disabilities, I became increasingly aware of how schools are designed to oppress many and privilege few. My students had serious problems that had been misdiagnosed and untreated. They, and their families, were poor, Black, and Latinx and caught up in multiple social service agencies. When they got to my school, they had already been kicked out of every other NYC District 75 placement. Their problems manifested themselves in aggressive behaviors because adults had not been able to serve them properly. The juvenile justice system, child protective services, foster care, mental health services, and public schools were not equipped to address their deep issues. I was charged with preparing them for the Global Studies Regents, the subject test that all students in New York State had to pass to get a Regents diploma. I had no teaching degree yet, but enough undergraduate credits in both English and history to qualify for a provisional license. My experience in California and my bachelor's degree were enough for NYC to determine that the least experienced teacher was qualified enough to serve the most vulnerable students. This was a systems design issue, and it set me on a lifelong journey of seeking to fix the very underpinnings of how we use public dollars to support the actions of adults who are supposed to make things better for youth.

Interestingly, this was also the advent of Teach for America (TFA), whose whole theory of action is that smart and passionate college graduates can serve students in low-income communities better than their traditionally prepared colleagues. I've known some great former TFAers who stayed as educators and became committed to the work. But the effect on actual students of this experiment is mixed, at best, while the idea captured the imagination of philanthropists, policy makers, and the media. It's a perfect example of how education has been caught up in simplistic solutions when the realities of change are so much more complex. This is why I've written this book.

Public schools have never served all children equally or equitably. This has been tacitly understood as a condition of American life, although lawsuits and major court cases have exposed resource inequities and led to some changes. Until No Child Left Behind (NCLB), achievement differences among student groups simply weren't measured or made apparent in the way they are now. This condition has thus become an organizing principle for school improvement over the last generation, although little progress has been made at scale. I became a system leader at the beginning of the NCLB era and watched first-hand as educators struggled to help schools improve. We tried various strategies such as mandating new curriculum, increasing site-based autonomy, or creating new rules and regulations. Some worked, others didn't. What has become abundantly clear is that there are no panaceas. This book rests on the idea that the role of a system leader is to help school leaders design, implement, and sustain comprehensive strategies for school improvement within the context of a district-wide transformation effort. I argue that while there can be a variety of approaches to improvement, there are core practices that system leaders can employ to ensure that schools are supported in that journey.

I've spent a lot of time considering the question of what keeps various initiatives from resulting in the desired outcomes, despite the promises of politicians and leaders. What can superintendents and their teams do differently that will result in real system transformation? Part of what I've come to realize in answering this question is the different worlds that system leaders and the public live in. The latter wants easily understood solutions to complex problems. They don't understand the underpinnings of how public-school districts have been constructed and how they work. They want their problems to be quickly solved by the people who are paid from their tax dollars and have little tolerance for explanations about why it may not be as easy as they think. Superintendents and system leaders, on the other hand, are engulfed in complexity. They would offer easy solutions when possible, but few things are. Equity, in particular, is an issue that has vexed us for far too long and doesn't lend itself to quick fixes or easy choices.

School system leaders need to address equity issues by organizing coherent strategies that embrace the complexity of change. Long-lasting change in public school systems doesn't come from implementing a new program with fidelity. Leaders who rely on a single initiative or product, such as the purchase of new technology (e.g., iPads) or a change in structure (e.g., block scheduling), run the risk of wasting precious time and funding. Rather, superintendents must understand the complex formal and informal rules, processes, and structures that undergird the daily actions of thousands of adults within the system, and then rewrite those rules and build a new ecosystem to attend to the needs of today's schools, educators, and students. And they can't do it alone. Superintendents have to develop and guide their teams and engage stakeholders in collaborative change management processes that align the work of adults around a clear set of nonnegotiable equity and student achievement goals. Their focus must be on adult practice.

School district leaders must understand the key levers of the system that improve adult practice to better serve children. Students won't learn the skills and knowledge they need to thrive in their future unless adults start doing something differently. System leaders are essential to organizing processes and developing structures for schools to do just that. The assignment of teachers, for example, is one of the most important equity moves that leaders can make, as the best teachers should serve the most vulnerable students.[2] But when I've asked system leaders about their approach to equity, many will describe the workshops on antibias instruction or the book study on culturally relevant pedagogy. Those efforts to change beliefs are necessary underpinnings of an equity strategy, but they won't lead to transformation on their own. System leaders need to couple the adaptive work of changing belief systems with the technical work of rewriting the rules. If there is no change in the rules guiding the assignment of teachers to students, leaders are left with only wishful thinking that actions will change. By ensuring the best teachers are with the most vulnerable students, coupled with a deep investment in changing beliefs, system leaders are more likely to promote the kind of change they seek. Yet superintendents must understand and confront some of the reasons why the initial teacher assign-ment rules exist in the first place. Within schools and districts, wealthier parents tend to demand more highly qualified teachers. Union contracts can limit the authority of a principal or system leader to reassign teachers. Teacher evaluation processes don't always allow for the gathering of holistic data that can help a leader determine a teacher's true strengths and needs. This book delineates an approach to change management that will help leaders understand these dynamics in order to change them.

Despite the mixed results of the last twenty years of reform, funders, poli-cy makers, and practitioners are turning to new methodologies grounded in old ideas. While there are fewer claims of silver bullets, there's certainly con-tinued admiration of technology, career technical education, school choice, and racial integration. Some reformers are calling for increased attention to curriculum and pedagogy, which is welcome, but I fear that these continue to be structural solutions to instructional problems. We hear regularly that the jobs of tomorrow haven't even been invented yet, so we need to teach uni-versal skills adaptable to any occupation. But a classics-type education that focuses on knowledge acquisition may just be the key to helping our students achieve. And everything we thought we knew about reading instruction turns out to be wrong. These "if-there-were-just" arguments come in and out of vogue every so often, and the educator is left standing in the middle, having to make choices every day that affect their students. What's missing from these debates is the necessary attention to the various components of the systems by which adults come together every day to serve children. The rules by which these systems exist and the choices that leaders make cre-ate the conditions under which teachers teach, leaders lead, and students learn. Leaders, especially superintendents of schools, need to consider six entry points if they want to transform how students are taught and what they achieve. And they must understand how we got to where we are today.

A BRIEF HISTORY OF SCHOOL SYSTEM DESIGN

I remember reading Ray Callahan's classic 1962 study, *Education and the Cult of Efficiency*,[3] in graduate school and first beginning to understand the genesis of school systems being designed around Frederick Taylor's notions of scientific management. As Jal Mehta so aptly described in *The Allure of Order*,[4] school districts were designed for operational compliance. Prior to the 1990s, schools focused on teaching and learning while school boards, superintendents, and administrators ensured fiscal and operational efficiency and compliance. Yet these same systems were never designed to truly let schools lead teaching and learning. Collective bargaining agreements with teachers, efficient transportation schedules, consistent start and end times, bulk purchasing of materials, budget formulas, and staffing models all constrain the ability of schools to go beyond the district-determined approach to teaching and learning. Principals are then left to allocate the resources they've been given and manage their employees and communities within the guardrails that have been set up. The tension between the autonomy and decision-making power of the individual school and the strictures of the district is often referred to as the "loose–tight continuum."[5] This tension is the high wire that superintendents balance on when they're leading an equity-based transformation effort.

As Weick described in his classic paper and Elmore further delineated, school systems are controlled and managed by leaders who are disconnected from the actual work that happens within schools.[6] Thus, their actions are often discordant with what schools need in order to serve students well. When it comes to content—what students should know and be able to do and what adult capacities will help them achieve those standards—this loose–tight dynamic can be exacerbated and create more tension. School districts simply aren't organized to improve instruction and, in fact, hadn't been expected to do so until this last generation of reform. They were, however, designed to control from afar what front-line teachers were doing. During the Progressive Era, management "sought to shift power upwards from frontline workers (teachers) to administrative superiors, who would set goals, prescribe desired strategies, and use an early form of assessment to hold teachers accountable for their performance . . . expertise and hence power reside at the top rather than on the front line."[7] This kind of administrative control was rooted in patriarchal attitudes toward a female workforce combined with the latest thinking about efficient management. Moreover, historically, school systems were designed with the belief that resource allocation—books, teachers, supplies—would lead to outcomes, so central offices were responsible for that more than anything else.[8] Due to grave concerns about American students falling behind other those of other countries and thus compromising our economic competitiveness, the 1980s brought the beginning of the standards and accountability movement that we're still in today. According to Peurach et al.:

> The debates and compromises of the 1980s and early 1990s began to build consensus around operational conceptions that would soon drive federal and state policy. Excellence would center more narrowly on improving outcome measures for all students (and not privileging the success of some while neglecting others). Equity would center on reducing disparities in outcome measures among students, such that, as quality increased, gaps between students would narrow (and not sustain or expand). Realizing these ambitions, finally, would require comprehensive, coordinated initiatives aimed at transforming U.S. public education from an access-oriented mass public schooling enterprise to a collection of instructionally focused education systems.[9]

This movement culminated in the 2001 passage of No Child Left Behind (NCLB), forcing central offices to manage school improvement according to state accountability systems aligned to the new federal law. To comply with NCLB, districts increased investment in instructional support, technical assistance, and professional development,[10] which meant that system leaders had to increase their span of control. As such, they had to learn new skills. These new skills, however, were grounded in old mental models of compliance and monitoring. Moreover, the structures and functions of the central office didn't fundamentally change with the new work they were expected to do. Again, according to Peurach et al. (2019):

> It has also created new organizational categories that can be used to signal a positive responsive to excellence and equity though, again, without making deep changes in classroom instruction: for example, pursuing "21st-century skills" and "deeper learning" using "culturally responsive pedagogies" and "restorative practices" supported by "research-based," "research-validated," and "standards-aligned" curriculum materials, all under the guidance of "highly qualified teachers" engaged in "data-driven decision making" and "PDSA cycles" in "professional learning communities."[11]

This "signaling" of new work, combined with a single-minded focus on English language arts (ELA) and mathematics standardized test scores, has not led to significant improvement in student achievement, although there has been an increased investment in central offices to support programs and centralized management of improvement processes. Moreover, most are still organized under an old paradigm, even as they claim to be doing new work. Central offices are structured according to strict divisional responsibilities. Depending on the size of the system, the superintendent (who reports to an elected board of education) typically has a cabinet comprised of assistant superintendents who oversee various functions. Within operations/administration is usually housed finance, procurement, transportation, facilities and maintenance, food and nutrition, safety, and information technology. Human resources may sit within operations, although more and more we're seeing it as a stand-alone entity. On the instructional side of the house is curriculum and instruction, which usually contains content areas, special programs such as English language learners (ELLs) and special education, pupil personnel services, social emotional learning (SEL), federal title programs, and instructional technology. Oftentimes the office that deals with research, planning, and accountability reports up to the curriculum side of the house, as does the diversity, equity, and inclusion team (which may include community engagement), if there is one. Again, depending on the size of the district there may be an assistant superintendent or chief that supervises principals, or that could be the job of either the assistant superintendent of curriculum and instruction or the superintendent. I was a cabinet member in small district of eight thousand students and twelve schools, and superintendent of two districts, one with 15,500 students in twenty schools and the other with 154,000 in two hundred and two schools, and each system had a variation of what I described above.

Regardless of the composition and duties of the superintendent's cabinet and subsequent central office departments, the work itself is designed to be separate and distinct. Each assistant superintendent and their direct reports have a discrete job, reporting requirements, statutes and regulations, funding sources, and deliverables. Certainly, this logic is clear when serving food, transporting students, or maintaining school buildings. Such functions require consultation with school principals and coordination with other central office units but are largely independent. Yet those lines become a little fuzzier when considering the purchase of technology—both hardware and software—or recruiting and hiring teachers, or engaging with the community. Those functions should be aligned to the needs and visions of the various schools within the system. The supervision of principals is all too often a black box, wherein only the supervisor (superintendent, assistant superintendent, or some other official) and the supervisee have reviewed the data to determine progress, set new personal and professional goals, and develop a plan to help the school improve. Yet, as we will see, principal supervision is the lynchpin of a system-wide transformation effort.

The silos of central offices are not easily torn down. Most superintendents restructure their central offices early in their tenure as a symbol of the new regime and strategy. Job descriptions are rewritten, veteran administrators reapply for a position, and promises are made about how the new structure will lead to increased efficiency, effectiveness, accountability, and achievement. And then not much changes. Too little attention is paid to how these actors interact with each other and with schools every day to rewrite the rules. New job descriptions and titles won't by themselves attend to the complexity of transforming public school systems. They may offer an opportunity to bring in new talent or accelerate the implementation of an initiative. But they won't fundamentally change how the system works to serve children. But, as Honig and Rainey[12] have shown, it is possible to transform a central office around clear student learning and equity goals. The only way to truly transform public school systems, in my view, is by embracing that complexity and rewriting the rules of how leaders within the system come together around six entry points of transformation. This book is intended to help leaders do just that.

STRUCTURE OF THIS BOOK

This book is intended to provide K–12 public school system leaders guidance about how to transform their systems to improve teaching and learning through an equity lens. By describing an approach to change management that embraces the complexity of how public-school districts actually work, leaders will learn how to rewrite the rules of the systems in which students receive an education. My approach to change management is grounded in helping school system leaders use effective, research-based practices that promote equity and lead to improved student learning and achievement. I suggest that there are six entry points system leaders must attend to as they seek to transform the district. This book will focus on the complexity of the role that central office system leaders play in designing, implementing, and sustaining such efforts.

The six entry points in this book are based on my experience in school systems, my understanding of the literature, and my observations and knowledge of the work of superintendents and system leaders throughout the country. I've been doing this work for a while, and while I'd never suggest that these six should be the sole focus of a superintendent, I believe they're a good starting point. The rules that I suggest should be rewritten are meant to serve as examples. They're not an exhaustive list, as every district has its own context, history, and regulatory environment. Again, I'm suggesting that superintendents and system leaders need to ask questions about the written and unwritten rules that guide the daily actions of adults within their systems. Those actions will accelerate or stymie an equity agenda. I provide multiple examples of equity work that leaders have used, although I don't provide an exhaustive or definitive list of every successful equity move a leader can make. To my mind, the question is not whether a leader can describe the enaction of such practices and even get policies or budgets passed to support them. Rather, it is how they go about doing so that is the real test. Whatever the equity move may be, its success depends on the leader's strategy for implementation.

The first entry point I consider is teaching and learning, as that should be the main focus of school systems. That is the reason they exist. The rule that leaders must rewrite is about who gets access to what kind of instruction. The standards movement of the last thirty years has led to changes in how students are taught and the content they're exposed to. Schools have organized around Advanced Placement (AP), algebra by eighth grade, problem-based learning, and more recently career pathways. The essential question is who has access to that kind of higher level, engaging instruction. Too often it's white and Asian students who are placed in the most advanced courses and given opportunities to learn higher-level content. Students who are Black, Latinx, differently abled, English language learners, or poor aren't given the same opportunities. System leaders must start their transformation effort by focusing on that question.

The second entry point is values, as system leaders must focus on what we believe about adults and children. Every leader comes into their work with a set of values and beliefs about education and how change happens. And every community and school has their own values and approach to change. Transformation efforts grounded in equity must navigate through these different values and beliefs about how change should happen and who actually needs to change. The rule that needs to be rewritten is about how leaders engage stakeholders in processes that create a set of shared values to organize system-wide change. Those shared values are the foundation for strategic planning and the development of language that reflects high aspirations for students. Moreover, leaders must first "know thyself" and make their values and stories clear to their community. By authentically doing so they inspire others to follow their lead.

The third entry point is decision-making. Leaders need a clear understanding of where formal and informal power lies. An equity-based transformation agenda requires superintendents to be clear about who gets to make what kinds of decisions. The rule that needs to be rewritten is one of transparency and engagement. System leaders don't have the power to make every decision. They can use their influence, they can inspire, they can cajole, and they can push and pull people along. But determinations about who gets taught what and how, the allocation of resources to support the system's vision and needs, and how talent gets distributed are made with and by others throughout the system. Leaders need to be transparent about how those decisions get made, the data used to inform them, and the intended outcomes. In addition, comprehensive engagement processes that activate stakeholder voices are essential components of an equity agenda.

The fourth entry point is resource allocation. Leaders need to attend to how time is spent, talent is distributed, and money is allocated according to the system's vision and needs. Leaders spend an enormous time on getting a spending plan passed by the board of education, taxpayers, and the local funding authority. Yet, funds aren't the only way to think about resources. How educators spend their time every day, and which educators serve the most vulnerable students, are essential ingredients of an equity agenda. The rule that needs to be rewritten is both simple and complex. Leaders must ensure that those who need the most get the most. This is easier said than done, given the complexity of public school systems.

The fifth entry point is talent management. People not only comprise more than 80 percent of a school district's budget, they're also the most powerful equity tool that a superintendent has. System leaders need to focus on the people who are actually doing the work every day with students. No program, policy, or technology will mean anything if the people who interact with students, families, and educators aren't supported, developed, and held to a high standard. The rules that need to be rewritten concern systems of recruitment, collective learning, and support of the educators within the system. Equity-based transformation agendas also require that attention is paid to increasing employee diversity.

The sixth entry point is culture. Leaders need to understand the unwritten rules of the context they're in and how people feel and act within the organization. How people interact with each other every day in service of young people and families is the foundation of improvement. An improvement culture requires that people grapple with hard truths and make collective decisions about how to achieve goals and address needs. Establishing the trust needed to sustain an improvement culture is work that only the superintendent can do, even as they inherit extant cultures. The rule that needs to be rewritten is simply about paying explicit attention to culture while modelling what a leader wants to see others do.

In the seventh and final chapter I try to tie everything together. I offer some practical strategies and moves that system leaders can make to drive an equity agenda. Again, these are not meant to be conclusive or exhaustive. Rather, they are ways to organize collective effort to transform public school systems so that more students achieve a higher standard.

Each chapter consists of some of my personal stories as a system leader, references to relevant literature, and depictions of leaders who have done the work. The leaders I chose to profile in this book have had varying degrees of success as superintendents. I intentionally spoke to people I have watched lead over the year in different roles and various contexts. Some have had great success as superintendents; others have struggled. And that's part of why I wanted to write this book. Leaders are made of their successes and their failures. If a leader has never failed, it's probably because they were too timid and cautious. An equity agenda requires bold action and difficult decisions. The complexity of organizing collective action in a highly politicized and regulated environment cannot be overstated. Superintendents who choose to take on such work do so because they feel a sense of urgency that adults can do better by young people. Sometimes that urgency to act is thwarted by the conditions and actors on the ground. Yet, even if a leader hasn't been able to see their work to its full fruition, they can still embrace the complexity and rewrite the rules so that children are better served in our public schools.

1

Start with Teaching and Learning

STEVE LEINWAND MOVED across the room, arms flailing about, his energy growing with every algebraic expression he put on the whiteboard. Teachers were starting to nod their heads and sit up a little straighter, trying to capture his wisdom about how to teach algebra to all students. Steve's message about conceptual understanding being equally important to operational execution had gotten their attention. His focus on teacher knowledge, skills, and creativity was resonating too. Perhaps algebra wasn't just about memorization. The effort to overhaul mathematics instruction in the Stamford Public Schools wasn't going to be about simply implementing a canned curriculum with fidelity. Perhaps the new superintendent was actually doing what he said he believed in, using teacher expertise and collaborative, professional learning to improve their skills in order to help more students achieve standards. Maybe this time would be different.

We had brought Steve into Stamford as part of our middle school transformation initiative. The General Electric (GE) Foundation had started a national initiative to invest in urban school systems where they had a big presence, and their corporate offices were in our area. The funds were intended to drive improvement in our K–12 science, technology, engineering, and math (STEM) offerings, as this was 2006 and STEM was becoming the North Star for many districts throughout the country. The GE Foundation was not requiring us to adopt a distinct program or curriculum. Rather, they were interested in our systemic approach to transformation. We had to have a clear strategy for improving teaching and learning, and we had to get results. They pushed us on both the strategy and the implementation, as the "say–do" ratio is one of their organizing principles. If a leader says they're going to do something, they better do it. Middle school was the most distinctly inequitable entity in the district, as manifested in the rigid tracking of students into academic groups. So we decided to focus our energies there.

This chapter is about content and how leaders can leverage curriculum as an entry point for system transformation. By content I mean what people do every day in service of students. How do schools ensure that students are learning what they need to be successful in the twenty-first century, and how do leaders develop the capacities of adults to help each student succeed? The problem American public schools are trying to solve is to graduate every student with the knowledge, skills, and abilities to embrace an increasingly complex world on their own terms. To solve this, problem students must develop a skill set and learn content that is relevant to their futures. If task predicts performance, then what are teachers asking of students in classrooms?

There are three rules about the student experience that need to be rewritten when focusing on teaching and learning: access, standards, and expectations. There is one rule about adults that needs to be rewritten, that of teacher leadership. Too many school systems are still designed to rank and sort young people, even if they claim the mantle of equity. Leaders need to ensure that the system is redesigned so that all students have access to the kind of high-quality, standards-based instruction that will prepare them to embrace their futures. When it comes to transforming school systems so that more students have that kind of access, those who are closest to the problem should be deeply involved in solving it. This means that teachers need to be leading the work. This chapter is focused on the reasons why such changes need to be made and introduces themes that are discussed further in subsequent chapters.

For 180 days, seven hours a day, students are in classrooms and schools with adults. What they're asked to accomplish during that time is the core of every adult's work and reflects the values of both the individual school and the system as a whole. Whether kindergarten students are engaged in structured play and social-emotional skill development or are being prepared for state kindergarten readiness assessments in reading and math reflects a system's values and its beliefs about which students are capable of learning certain material. Perhaps high school students are graded according to common assessments in core subject areas, or their individual teachers have autonomy to determine their grades. Maybe a school system has invested in texts and units of study that reflect the diversity of their student populations. School systems have to be organized around a clear picture of what students should know and be able to do and the skills, knowledge, and dispositions that adults need to help them achieve those goals. Content is the bread and butter of school systems.

In truly diverse school systems with a majority of traditionally underserved students, what is learned on a daily basis is the crux of one of the biggest challenges we have in public education. In too many diverse school systems, white, Asian, and affluent students take more rigorous and higher-level courses than do Black and Latinx students, students with disabilities (SWDs), English language learners (ELLs), and poor students. In systems with a preponderance of the latter types of students, advanced options like Advanced Placement or International Baccalaureate might not even be available.[1] Yet schools and districts are held to the same academic standards within state accountability systems, and most students are trying to get into college. What we do every day with students reflects our values and beliefs, and if educators purport to be acting through an equity lens, it should be evident in the kind of content they provide to students, the standards on which that content is based, and access to that content.

I use mathematics as an example of the rules that bind diverse school systems in inequitable practices and make transformation that much more complex. Through my experience in Stamford, Connecticut; Brian Osborne's work in South Orange Maplewood, New Jersey; and Joe Davis's leadership of Ferguson-Florissant, Missouri, I highlight how superintendents have used content as a lever for change. In Stamford, our detracking work was grounded in community engagement, teacher leadership, and explicit changes to policy. Many rules were rewritten in order to increase equity and access. Under the leadership of Brian Osborne, the South Orange Maplewood School District went through a similar detracking effort and provides another example of how to leverage content as the foundation of a system transformation effort. Joe Davis in Ferguson-Florissant has shown that a focus on mathematics can improve the achievement and experience of Black students in particular.

THE EQUITY IMPERATIVE

Stamford, Connecticut is a city of about 125,000 citizens in the southeastern part of the state. It's a hub in its own right, with corporate headquarters and many businesses, while also being a suburb for commuters to New York City. In the 1960s, in the face of growing diversity, the Stamford Board of Education and community decided that it would voluntarily integrate the schools. The plan contained aspects typical of diverse districts seeking to voluntarily integrate: build magnet schools in more diverse urban parts of town to attract white students and set a policy that all schools would reflect the overall demographics of the county within 10 percentage points above or below the average of total minority students. A complementary system was put in place so that while students of different ethnicities would be in the same schools, they wouldn't be in the same classes. Hard and fast rules were created to entrench white supremacy, even as the powers that be claimed to be progressive in desiring desegregated schools.

The Stamford Board of Education set policy in the early 1970s establishing the Cooperating Groups System (COGS).[2] A standardized test score placed a student in a COG, and then the cohort would stay with the same set of teachers. Placement was determined by a "Z score"—a composite of a student's fifth-grade math and English language arts standardized test scores. The result was that the COGS reflected the demographic distribution of the scores. Black and Hispanic students, whose scores were lower than white students (there were few Asians at the time), were placed in the same COGS, thereby segregating classes. While this rule was explicit in Stamford, systems throughout the country have similar formal and informal sorting and selecting processes. In Stamford, tracking started informally in many elementary schools as early as kindergarten, despite a policy established in 1972 that elementary school classes would be heterogeneously grouped. Some principals were beholden to powerful white parents, often on the PTA, who wanted a certain teacher for their kids. Others were influenced by their teachers, who believed that it was in the best interest of their students to group them according to ability.

At the two comprehensive high schools in Stamford, tracking was manifest as a byproduct of what students received in middle school. All of the typical gates were up to sort students into levels of classes. Students were placed into honors—and then AP—through teacher recommendations, cut scores, guidance counselor judgement, and, of course, parental advocacy. Since Black and Latinx students were getting low-level instruction during middle school, they were placed in lower-level courses in high school. It was a self-fulfilling prophecy and a vicious cycle that no one considered breaking, as that was just the way it was in Stamford. The upshot is that while the Stamford community hailed its success at desegregating schools, it had simultaneously entrenched segregated classrooms.

Not only were Black and Latinx students denied access to higher-level courses, there were no standards for what students should know and be able to do, and little coherence in curriculum throughout the district. Every school was essentially allowed to operate according to its own vision for teaching and learning. This exacerbated the white privilege and entitlement that was rampant in Stamford, and it made it nearly impossible to hold educators accountable and establish school improvement systems. After all, without a clear set of standards and expectations for folks to organize around, what are they trying to achieve?

EMBRACE THE COMPLEXITY

During my interviews with the board, they asked me explicitly about my thoughts on heterogeneous grouping. I knew the basic research exposing the perniciousness of tracking students. I had also worked previously in a district of nearly all Black and Latinx students that had successfully increased student achievement by raising standards, overhauling curriculum, investing in social emotional learning, and providing comprehensive professional learning for educators. The evidence on what helps students achieve at high levels is pretty clear—raising expectations, not lowering them. Thus, the distinct tracks in Stamford reflected a culture and system of low expectations for the most vulnerable students, and this was not a recipe for success. I also knew that this would be my "hill to die on." Every superintendent who's truly seeking to transform a system through an equity lens knows they're going to face a lot of opposition. For many leaders, the fear of that opposition leads to placing safe bets instead of taking bold action that rewrites the rules. As Rudy Crew, who led New York City and Miami, once told me, you know you're going to get fired eventually, so you might as well choose what you get fired for.

Fortunately, I had the lever of No Child Left Behind (NCLB) to provide the urgency and catalyst for change. I had serious concerns about NCLB, as it led to narrowing curriculum and elevating flawed standardized tests in English language arts (ELA) and mathematics as the only measures of success. Yet, NCLB also served a powerful purpose by making public the vast differences in student achievement, even if the measure was limited. There was simply no escaping the fact that white students in America were achieving at much higher levels than Black and Latinx students. It was proof that the system was not serving all children well. NCLB also forced educators to learn how to use data. There are legitimate arguments to be made that the utility of standardized test score data is limited and that the obsession with these scores has hurt schools and education as a whole. Yet, if state standardized test scores are seen as a floor, not a ceiling, then schools and systems can use them as starting points for further analysis to determine what students really need. Good leaders make opportunities out of crises, and there was no denying that the test scores of students in Stamford reflected a crisis.

Tracking provided a moral imperative, and NCLB was a requirement that we needed to address. Thus, there was a clear mandate to make systemic changes in both how and what students were being taught. The question, though, was how to go about transforming the system. Eliminating formal and informal tracks and ensuring that all students, K–12, had access to high-quality instruction every single day required that we touch every part of the district. Improving instruction is not just about buying new curriculum or providing teachers with professional learning. Accountability systems won't improve teaching and learning by measuring outcomes, nor will inspiring or threatening pronouncements from superintendents. The only way to change student outcomes is to focus on what adults are doing every day with students. As Richard Elmore liked to say, task predicts performance. By focusing on the learning that students are engaged in every day, leaders can begin to transform schools and districts. It's as straightforward, and as complex, as that.

REWRITING THE RULES

To make fundamental, systemic change to teaching and learning, I knew I needed to focus on entrenched components of the system in addition to classroom instruction. The support of the GE Foundation enabled me to accelerate this work. I was able to spend foundation money on a PDK curriculum audit of our elementary literacy program, which is a comprehensive analysis of the entire instructional management system. The audit reviews governance, policy, and resource allocation in addition to curriculum alignment to standards and observation of actual instruction. The auditors found more than one hundred approaches to literacy among twelve elementary schools, which gave the impetus to start changing what and how we taught students to read. It also enabled the start of a policy conversation with the board. I was interested in pursuing an equity policy, as I wanted to codify a new approach to better serving all students and ensuring the most vulnerable got the resources and support they needed. Equity policies were rare back then, and I was concerned about the politics of trying to move something like that through. So, we initiated a change to the curriculum policy itself. It was updated to clearly state that all students must have access to standards-based instruction, among other things.[3] While this may seem like an obvious thing for a school system to require, tracking and homogeneous grouping of students, with commensurate low-level instruction, made it so that only some students were given access to standards-based instruction. This policy change, along with NCLB and the support of the GE Foundation, created a context for us to start overhauling what and how students were learning. It also made it that much more difficult for the small but intense group of resistors to push back.

Whenever a leader changes the fundamental underpinnings of an inequitable system, resistance is inevitable. The white people who have always benefited from the rules that have privileged their children don't like it when their entitlement is compromised. In Stamford, a small group of politically powerful white parents organized an effort to thwart the changes I was trying to make. But I had a board policy to follow. And, I had worked very hard to mobilize leaders and stakeholders in the community who had not previously been engaged. The NAACP, community groups, parents of color, and Latinx leaders were starting to pay attention to what we were doing. White allies were also starting to speak up in support of detracking. By engaging the community, we were breaking the traditional power structure that held Stamford in its grasp for so long and had prevented substantive change. We were also rewriting the rule that only some parents should have their voices heard when undoing the inequities of a school system.

The decision to focus on math was driven both by the support of the GE Foundation and a clear and compelling equity imperative. Math has been, and continues to be, one of the primary gatekeepers in American public education. In many districts with diverse populations, students are formally and informally separated at an early age for math instruction. Some, typically white and Asian, are designated to be on a math pathway that leads to Algebra 1 by eighth grade, or even earlier. Others, typically Black and Latinx, don't take Algebra 1 until ninth grade. Algebra 1 by eighth grade has come to symbolize the equity problem in schools and has even been referred to as a civil rights issue. Advanced math and science courses in high school leads to admission into more selective colleges and universities. In order to take advanced math courses, such as calculus and AP, as well as some higher-level science courses, students need to have taken Algebra 1 by eighth grade. Thus, if you're not in Algebra 1 by eighth grade, you're not on a path to admission into more selective colleges. Stamford's tracking system essentially guaranteed that the only students who would take Algebra 1 in eighth grade and be on a path to more advanced math and sciences in high school would be white and Asian.

Our efforts to change math instruction rested on two core stakes in the ground. One was about equity and access, in that only some students were getting adequate math instruction that prepared them for college and career. The second was about pedagogy and teacher content knowledge, as instruction was too grounded in memorization without enough problem solving and conceptual understanding. We wanted students to be engaged and have fun as they tackled complex problems. And we knew that we had to start at elementary school, as that's where a student first forms their math identity, and where too many teachers are able to half-jokingly state, "Oh, I'm not a math person," as they struggle with new curriculum. Transforming math instruction had to start with teachers and their sense of efficacy.

Thus, we started by engaging teachers in setting standards, reviewing and choosing curriculum for district-wide adoption, and leading collaborative professional learning communities (PLCs). We were changing the rule of who gets to determine changes to teaching and learning by having teachers lead the way.

About forty teachers were involved in our mathematics think tank. The theory behind it was pretty simple: Those who were closest to the problem we were trying to solve should be heavily involved in developing solutions. There were political reasons too. Parents tend to trust teachers more than they do the superintendent and central office. Changing mathematics instruction can be a big risk, given the entitlement many white parents feel toward advanced math and the assumptions they make about what good math instruction looks like, largely based on their own experiences of being ranked and sorted. Unhappy parents tend to complain to elected officials, who can then slow down the implementation or decrease funding. Additionally, the leadership of the Stamford teacher's union had a history of opposing almost any change. Thus, I wanted rank-and-file teachers to be champions of the new approach so that the union leadership wouldn't go against its own members. I needed teachers to vouch for the legitimacy of our decision and the process by which we came to it.

The think tank was charged with determining standards and best practices and setting a vision for district-wide K–12 math instruction. Given the vast differences in the approaches to teaching and learning that schools had taken over the years, this was the first time that many teachers had an opportunity to learn about what their colleagues were doing. In fact, this was the first time many teachers had even met peers from other schools. One of the unintended benefits of this kind of collective leadership and decision-making was that a community of professional colleagues found sustenance and support in each other. The teachers who joined the think tank tended to be intellectually curious and informal leaders in their schools. They were the teachers who would go above and beyond and try out new techniques and practices. Such teachers can sometimes feel lonely and isolated in their schools if their peers don't share their approach to the work. In the think tank they found community. These teachers also had the opportunity to work directly with central office leaders, including myself, as

I tried to participate in meetings as much as possible. Many of the participants went on to become school and system leaders in Stamford during my time there and after I left.

The think tank settled on a few key principles to transforming mathematics instruction. They determined appropriate standards based on both Connecticut state standards and National Council of Teachers of Mathematics (NCTM), the professional association for math teachers. They believed in a spiraled rather than scaffolded curriculum, which allowed for regular reviews of concepts and operations. Professional learning was seen as essential, as were monitoring, feedback, and support. We also put in place common assessments throughout the district so that there would be a consistent basis of comparison in order to help us learn and improve. Most important to the think tank were equity issues. Everyone knew that we had a serious problem when it came to how students were tracked and how that placement not only segregated students but relegated students of color to an inadequate education. By tackling the transformation of mathematics instruction, we were able to start reconstructing a system that had oppressed many and privileged few for generations.

Not only did student achievement increase in elementary and middle school grades, but the high schools started opening access to Advanced Placement classes. Within six years, by the time I left to become superintendent of Montgomery County, Maryland, there were no more rigid tracks for students, curriculum reflected a higher standard and was consistent across the district, we had put in place a comprehensive approach to professional learning, a multimeasure accountability system had been established, and all students had access to higher-level courses in high school. By focusing on content—what students learn every day and who gets access to what—we had transformed the Stamford public schools.

EQUITY, ACCESS, AND COHESION

Dr. Brian Osborne became superintendent of schools in South Orange Maplewood (SOMA), New Jersey, in 2007. The year prior to his arrival students and teachers at the high school had walked out in protest of racially insensitive comments the principal had made. Osborne's predecessor had supported the principal, but a Board of Education election brought new members and then a new superintendent to this suburban New Jersey district comprised of 50 percent Black and 50 percent white students. When the Board selected Osborne they were looking for someone who could help them heal and move forward in a thoughtful and strategic way.

At thirty-seven years old, Brian Osborne hadn't been a principal but had worked in senior-level positions in New York City and other school districts. A Teach for America alum who taught math as part of the founding team for a new school in the South Bronx, Osborne had a deep commitment to both equity and the need for all kids to be in classrooms with high expectations. His experience in the Bronx opened his eyes to the stark realities of American public school, and he knew that his students were just as smart as any others but didn't have the same opportunities. Having grown up in suburban Oak Park, Illinois, Osborne knew the ecosystem of excellence that surrounded them was the difference-maker. Expectations to attend college and support from families and schools almost guaranteed success for suburban students and was woefully absent in the Bronx. When Osborne became superintendent, he knew that the key was for every student in SOMA to have good instruction, in every class, every day from K–12. Those simple principles about access and standards were the foundations of his transformation effort and the rules he needed to rewrite.

Like most diverse districts, even well-resourced suburban ones where many recent transplants from the city celebrate diversity, students in SOMA had different experiences depending on their demographics. When Osborne arrived, there was only half-day kindergarten. The remainder of the day was, of course, supplemented by wealthier parents who could afford for their child to have an enriching experience. By first grade, the gaps between students were evident and continued throughout their elementary years. Thus, establishing full-day kindergarten became Osborne's first major equity campaign. In order to do so he had to convince the citizens, as it was a ballot question on the annual budget vote. He had to ensure board approval, allocate appropriate funding, find adequate space, and earn the support of teachers. It wasn't clean, however, as there were space limitations, which meant that Osborne had to restrict the number of students who could attend. He decided to prioritize students receiving free and reduced-price meals, which didn't sit well with some parts of the community and decreased his political capital.

Curriculum cohesion in kindergarten was a key part of his strategy. Doubling the amount of time that students were spending in class meant that teachers needed to keep them engaged, safe, and learning much longer than they were used to. This was also during the period when states were beginning to assess readiness in the early grades, and some were arguing that kindergarten was becoming the new first grade. Parental expectations that their child become a fluent reader by age five or six can complicate matters, as a lot of early childhood research concludes that structured play and social-emotional development are the key ingredients for a successful kindergarten program. Osborne had to navigate all of this complexity, which he did by involving the teachers deeply in the process. As the superintendent, he was the external and internal champion for this work. Osborne's success rested with the teachers, who he publicly and privately celebrated and resourced. He served as their cheerleader as they made curriculum changes, created new schedules, and generally led the work. When school started in September 2008, kindergartens were full of eager children learning and playing for a full day in classrooms with happy and skilled teachers. Osborne had successfully combined an equity imperative with a thoughtful approach to improving a child's daily experience. He had also rewritten the rule of who leads the work by having teachers out in front championing the change.

Brian Osborne's biggest initiative to transform SOMA was develeling the middle schools. In order to do this, he had to rewrite the rule of expectations. During his entry phase he spent a lot of time talking to students. At a lunch with a group of middle schoolers, he asked them what teachers expect of them. The answer could not have more clearly reflected the beliefs that too many adults had about students and the subsequent structures that calcified inequities. The students told Osborne that expectations of teachers depended on the level they were in, and that those levels were segregated by race. All of a sudden, Osborne was back in the South Bronx, faced with the realization that some students were expected to achieve at higher levels by virtue of their skin color, and it was okay to have lower expectations for Black students, even across the bridge in the suburbs. For Osborne, though, "The existence of lower-level courses themselves cements the expectation and the expectation becomes a self-fulfilling prophecy."[4] He knew that the students who are in higher levels think they're special, and vice versa for students in lower levels. Young people who are told they're smart regardless of having to work for the designation become afraid to take chances in their learning because they don't want to be exposed. And kids that are told they're not smart give up because the work is too low-level and it's clear that no one believes in them anyway.

Brian knew that the previous superintendent had taken some steps to change the rigidity of the levels in the system. While they didn't have a clear teaching and learning agenda, as evidenced from the lack of coherence across the system and absence of a solid ELA curriculum, they had deleveled sixth-grade courses except for math two years prior to Osborne's arrival. Absent a community engagement strategy and political capital, this change stirred controversy among parents. Lawn signs and a website claiming "Levels can Work" signaled the opposition that some white parents had to heterogeneous grouping in middle schools. And, as is typical in school districts, the board was split six-to-three in support of the change, and senior staff were nervous about upsetting the status quo (much of which they had supported and entrenched for years). Osborne describes the "transcript protectors" amid his central office who expressed concern that putting students they thought weren't ready into higher-level courses would affect their GPA and threaten their chances of getting into good colleges.

Too many diverse school systems have an unwritten rule of differentiated expectations. When few adults vocalize their beliefs about the abilities of students of color to learn high-level material, those expectations guide the establishment of formal and informal rules that bind too many students to low-level instruction. And when someone confronts those expectations, they can be met with reasoned counterarguments such as needing universal access to preK or enrichment programs at a young age so that more students can qualify for a specialized program—or the fears of parents who worry that their child's designation as advanced will be compromised if everyone is allowed to take upper-level courses is manifest in concerns about large class sizes, lack of individual attention, safety, or the inability of the teachers to give the kinds of significant support to the new students who used to be kept out of such classes.

Osborne made sure that despite the opposition of some white parents, the lack of support from a few board members, and the resistance of some on his team, the middle school principals were supportive of his efforts. Moreover, given his experience as a math teacher and his deep knowledge of and passion for the subject, he was ready to delevel mathematics. He therefore led the process to transform seventh-grade mathematics levels by moving to two from four and ending the practice of "microleveling." The district math supervisor had not only supported rigid levels in math, she helped the schools microlevel by creating classes of students with similar scores. Thus, within one level the class assignments would be based on a narrow range of scores, thereby further cementing the system. Some practices in schools are formal and obvious, while others hide behind the ongoing decision-making processes of school and system leaders (more on this in chapter 3). Brian was able to grasp both the de jure and de facto student assignment processes in SOMA middle schools and used that knowledge to drive change.

As Osborne spent the year deleveling seventh grade, including math, resistance grew on the board and in the community. But he had the data. Using recently available data that provided the ability to follow K–12 students into college, Brian used his analytic and political skills to show that students who were in lower-level courses did not fare well in higher education.[5] Armed with the data, and still having a majority on the board, Osborne was able to establish deleveling as policy. He had already shifted the board and district toward policy governance, which then gave him the impetus to get the board to take the standing policy dictating levels and course assignment processes out of their purview. He had to make a trade by having them approve subsequent changes in the program of studies, but he had effectively wrested control of the most glaring equity issue in the district. The "Aim Higher" slate running for the board in opposition to his transformation efforts weren't happy, but through extensive community engagement, thoughtful data analysis, and supportive school leaders, Osborne was able to transform teaching and learning in the middle schools.

MATHEMATICS INSTRUCTION AS THE SYMBOL OF EQUITY

Mathematics is a primary ranking and sorting mechanism for American public education in most public schools. Throughout the country students are labeled according to their proficiency in math at an early age, and they develop a commensurate identity as a "math person" or "not a math person." Elementary teachers echo these sentiments about themselves while simultaneously trying to teach students mathematics. While most districts have some form of accelerated or gifted studies in elementary school that separate students, formal segregation according to perceived ability typically starts in middle school. By the time students are in ninth grade, their math identity and options for various levels of courses are largely established. And while advanced mathematics can certainly lead to acceptance at more competitive universities and then well-paying jobs, we have been too satisfied for too long to allow a limited number of students to grab that brass ring.

It seems as if in every generation the lack of math achievement becomes a rallying cry for public school reform. In a 2016 report, "Mathematics Education in the United States,"[6] the NCTM describe three eras of math education since 1980. From 1980 to 1989, the United States was engaged in standard setting. Culminating in President George H. W. Bush's Goals 2000, politicians and industry leaders coalesced around the idea that American children needed to be taught content aligned to rigorous standards. For math, that meant that students would learn problem-solving, develop conceptual understanding behind the computations they performed, and use technology such as computers and calculators whenever possible and that assessments would go beyond the conventional, among other things.

The second phase of math reform these past forty years, according to NCTM, stretched from 1990 to 2009 and was all about implementation of the standards. A significant amount of focus was placed on both teacher preparation and knowledge as well as curriculum development and alignment. When NCLB became federal law in 2002 the stark gaps among student groups became abundantly clear to policy makers, business leaders, families, and educators. Subsequently, there was growing recognition of the lack of consistency of standards among states. The year 2010, then, saw the advent of the current third phase, that of Common Core State Standards (CCSS). Not unlike the tenets of the first phase thirty years prior, the CCSS in math advocated for problem solving, reasoning, communication, and collaboration.

Yet, despite grand pronouncements from elected officials, significant support from business leaders and philanthropists, new materials and resources from publishers and technologists, and most importantly, a major investment of time and effort on behalf of system leaders in school districts, American students' math performance remains mediocre. National Assessment of Educational Progress (NAEP) scores reveal that while there has been progress in grades four and eight since 1990, more than half of American students are not proficient in mathematics, and gaps persist between students in poverty and those who are not.[7] Twelfth-grade student scores have barely budged in the same amount of time. While NAEP is only one measure of student achievement, it's been the only consistent benchmark that American educators have had for thirty years.

Math instruction illustrates the challenges that system leaders face because it shows how difficult it can be to make real change in public school systems. Despite a compelling challenge, aligned policy, investment in professional learning, and abundant resources from the marketplace, mathematics achievement hasn't moved nearly as much as one might expect, given the attention paid to it. One could argue that we're using the wrong measures. The overreliance on standardized tests has done a disservice to our children and stifled exactly the kind of transformation in teaching that's required to enable more students to perform better in math. There's also an argument to be made that the current scaffolded approach to teaching math that follows a sequence determined more than one hundred years ago is simply not relevant to today.[8] There's certainly legitimacy to both of these arguments. Yet there's little evidence to suggest that if system leaders were to choose to either disregard standardized measures or overhaul the standard mathematics course sequence they would actually transform their system to better effect. What's missing from this puzzle is the nature of the system itself and how it's been designed and perpetuated for purposes that are very different from those that seed transformation.

THE NORTH STAR OF AP CALCULUS

Joe Davis wasn't planning on leaving his small North Carolina district. Having risen through the ranks in the area from bus driver, to math teacher, to principal, to superintendent, he and his family had it good. Joe had always been the kind of superintendent who led with his reason, intellect, and deep understanding of teaching and learning. But then Michael Brown was killed in Ferguson, Missouri, and soon after, the school district needed a new superintendent of schools. Joe's passion and anger were awakened, and he knew that he had to go to Ferguson-Florissant to lead that system.

When Joe became superintendent of Ferguson-Florissant, the district of approximately eleven thousand students—mostly Black, with about 11 percent white—needed more than healing. As a Black man who grew up with a single mother, Joe could identify with many of the young people in his schools. But Joe wasn't satisfied to simply focus on making people feel better in the aftermath of Michael Brown's death. While he knew that was important, he also had a deep commitment to the idea that healing was only part of the job. The rest of the work needed to be focused on teaching and learning. And for Joe Davis, that meant a relentless focus on mathematics.

Joe began his tenure by having a transition team of experts review the district. Unsurprisingly, they found that there were significant equity issues regarding student access to higher-level courses. The small number of white students were much more likely to be identified as gifted in elementary, enroll in Algebra 1 by eighth grade, and then take AP courses than most of the Black students. When the transition report was presented to the public, the community began to understand how the design of the Ferguson-Florissant system was doing a disservice to large swaths of students. Joe's board was fully behind him, so he set out to redesign how and when students would be engaged in a higher level of math instruction.

For Joe Davis, his passion and expertise when it came to mathematics gave him credibility with educators in the system. He not only spent a lot of time observing courses and talking to teachers, he would teach courses and model good instruction. He even delivered mathematics professional development to principals. As he started to restructure his team and ensure the right principals were in place, he laid the groundwork for a three-pronged strategy that began with the end in mind. If scoring a five on the AP Calculus test was the North Star, then the system needed to (1) improve teacher content knowledge in mathematics, especially in the elementary schools; (2) be grounded in a rich, standards-based curriculum; and (3) improve pedagogy so that students were engaged in problem solving and conceptual understanding. But Joe also knew that focusing on teaching and learning wouldn't be enough. He would have to change hearts and minds too.

Ferguson-Florissant, like many districts, has a lot of white female teachers who don't live in the community they serve. Being a white outsider doesn't automatically mean that there's a disconnect between you and your students, but it can certainly exacerbate extant societal divides. Joe could see that too many teachers simply didn't believe in their students. Just as Brian Osborne saw that high expectations are the foundation of rigorous instruction, Joe Davis knew that his teachers needed to believe that their students could achieve at a higher level if they were to meet his expectations around mathematics. And he knew that just telling teachers to do so wouldn't work; he needed to build their confidence in their ability to help all students. After all, if they hadn't been asked to teach differently, and hadn't been taught how to change their practice, how could they be expected to just embrace the new way and succeed at it? Joe channeled Richard Elmore's notion of reciprocal accountability: A leader can't hold someone accountable for something they don't know how to do, so a leader has to provide the opportunity to learn new skills.[9]

Beyond modelling lessons for principals, Joe focused on back-mapping standards and content from AP Calculus to elementary mathematics. While he knew that not every student would achieve a five on the exam, he wanted that clear expectation to permeate the system. Joe engaged the elementary school teachers in an effort to revamp report cards to be standards-based, as he wanted everyone to see what students were supposed to master at each level. He also focused his energy on principal supervision, as he knew that they were the key to transformation. By providing them with clear metrics and stakes in the ground to organize around, he struck the right balance on the "loose–tight" continuum.

After six years in Ferguson-Florissant, the work isn't close to done. Joe is now engaging the community more deeply than he has before, and he has to relentlessly focus on ensuring a culture of high expectations for Black children. But the numbers are steadily going up (the four-year graduate rate has increased to 91 percent), and as Joe has rewritten the rules around what his students can achieve, the Ferguson-Florissant school system is being transformed.

CONCLUSION

The transformation of a school system so that it better serves the most vulnerable students is a complex undertaking. As we'll see in the following chapters, there are multiple drivers of a comprehensive strategy that a system leader must employ. Yet the process starts with a clear vision for teaching and learning and by asking the questions, "What are students doing every day, for seven hours a day, one-hundred and eighty days a year?" and "Do adults have the requisite skills to serve all of our children to a high standard?" With those questions as the stake in the ground, leaders must then rewrite the rules of access, standards, and expectations. Then they must organize the rewriting process through extensive engagement. System leaders have a responsibility to deeply engage internal and external communities in the process of building a vision for teaching and learning while simultaneously articulating a clear one to students, families, educators and staff, and the community. And they must do so through an equity lens and a social justice stance. The former requires that a system leader ask whether and how the system maintains barriers of oppression; the latter mandates that a system leader dismantle those barriers.

A compelling vision for teaching and learning need not stand on its own, as state and federal laws borne of political considerations can be of great service to a system leader seeking to make change. Whether it was "A Nation at Risk," Goals 2000, NCLB, or the CCSS, savvy system leaders know how to use the political and legislative milieu to spark and demand change in their district. I used NCLB in Stamford to push for change, just as Brian Osborne did in SOMA. Superintendents can take the tack of compliance and simply organize their system to do what the laws require and what the politicians and funding demand, like making adequate yearly progress (AYP) every year. Or they can use it as an impetus to go beyond the minimum requirements and reimagine the possibilities within their schools. The most effective system leaders do the latter, although they often pay for bucking the status quo. Often, the leaders who last the longest do the former, even if it means dancing around the edges of equity.

Transformative system leaders will use various forms of data to help internal and external stakeholders understand why the proposed changes must happen. Brian Osborne's strategic use of data exposed the realities of college attainment and success for his students who take different levels of classes. That reality helped galvanize a community to understand the ultimate outcome of their system and the need for change. A leader can go even further by back-mapping to see which students were exposed to different teachers and how that effected their future achievement, which can then help schools understand patterns of teaching and learning within their schools. Or, like Joe Davis, a system leader can set a standard for students' ultimate achievement, such as a five on the AP calculus test, and then build a clear roadmap of what students should know and be able to do throughout their K–12 experience. External audits can be conducted to determine whether all students have equitable access to an instructional environment that will enable them to reach those goals. Equally powerful, teachers can be involved in peeling back the layers of the teaching and learning onion and be engaged in the transformation effort. There is a myriad of information that system leaders need to use to convince their stakeholders of the need for change and help focus collective efforts on what is most urgent, rather than just important.

System leaders need a political strategy as they transform their system. The "Big P" politics of elected officials, funding authorities, formal coalitions, and community groups must be attended to regularly. There may be some horse-trading and negotiating as budgets are set and initiatives are begun. The effective system leader must know when to push, when to pull, and when to wait, even if it sometimes means not moving as fast as they'd like. Leaders must build allies in the community as they work the politics through a "small p" strategy of knowing who has whose ear, who on their team has deep relationships with others in the district or community, and where both resistance and support may come from within schools and central offices. School districts are deeply political places with educators jockeying for power all the time, and since superintendents don't often stay as long as the lifers within a system, they have to be mindful of where the political potholes lie.

Finally, a comprehensive strategy for transforming teaching and learning rests on activating people who are closest to the issue as problem solvers. Central office leaders must be taught, supported, and held accountable for working in concert with formal and informal school leaders on instructional improvement efforts. There is a role for leadership from the top, but it is those who are closest to children and who are charged with serving them every day who must change their practice. They must be deeply engaged in the effort to design and implement the intended change. Not only will the initiative be better and have the potential to stick, because it reflects the real concerns and visions of those who are doing the work of teaching and learning, but it also provides political cover for system leaders, as the community and parents tend to trust their teachers more than their superintendent.

Rewriting the rules of who gets access to which content is at the core of a systems transformation effort. Equity and social justice will not be achieved without adults changing their perspectives on who deserves the best in the system and changing their practice to support all students attaining those standards. Great leaders embrace that complexity by applying their passion and vision in a methodical, data-based, and strategic way.

2

Values Drive the Work

PUBLIC SCHOOL SYSTEM transformation often happens amid both outrage and apathy. Low student achievement, the inability to make long-lasting fundamental change, petty political debates, and perhaps even the corruption of top officials can plague districts large and small. Outrage sparks call for change and new leadership, with subsequent promises to clean house and bring a new day of excellence, equity, and accountability. Apathy is found in the day-to-day existence of teachers, students, families, and community members who shrug their shoulders at the latest dysfunction while they keep on doing their jobs and sending their kids to school.

A leader who has a clear mandate for change must balance between these poles. They will need to both embrace the outrage as fuel and spur the apathetic to act. Balance is achieved within the political context of the district and the history of past reform efforts. A top-down approach that sweeps out the old and brings in the new is often found in larger urban settings with the election of a new mayor. It can be harder to overhaul a smaller system as the traditions, histories, and relationships are deep. The context of a smaller system can be confining for a new leader, with less room to maneuver than in larger systems. Regardless of district size, a new leader who wants to motivate the outraged and the apathetic to embrace change needs to be authentic by making their own values apparent. They must also rewrite the rules by appealing to shared values and inviting others to join a movement.

In order to transform a school system through an equity lens and a social justice stance, a leader needs to be both clear in what they believe in and willing to engage stakeholders around a set of shared values. Leaders need a strong core to steady them and a phalanx of supporters to protect them during difficult times. Political entities, such as a board or mayor, play roles as well, as they authorize change and can accelerate or stymie its pace. But for true transformation to take place, one where equity becomes embedded into the DNA of the system, a leader needs to engage others around a common set of values, and they need to ensure that adult actions reflect and reinforce those values.

Organizing school system transformation efforts around shared values is standard operating procedure. Leithwood notes that a key component of successful districts is a shared commitment to a vision, mission, and goals grounded in core values understood by everyone.[1] Kanter has shown how businesses with strong core values are able to quickly pivot and succeed in the face of new market conditions.[2] Values are both organizing and accountability principles. System leaders who are new to a district bring with them their own experiences and beliefs, and they must engage governing bodies, formal partners, and stakeholders to embrace a new set of shared values upon which to transform the system. Visions and missions are put forth as maypoles to rally around, and plans are developed to organize the implementation and measure results. These rules are necessary, but they're not sufficient. Leaders must also make their own values known to their community if they want to motivate people to commit, not just comply.

This chapter suggests that a leader must rewrite the rules through deep stakeholder engagement and a focus on values. Entry, transition work, and strategic planning processes are opportunities for leaders to organize efforts to use shared values to change adult actions in service of students. These processes also ensure that transformation happens within the context and culture of the community. This chapter describes how a leader's values can negatively and positively influence school systems. In the New York City Department of Education, Joel Klein's leadership exemplifies how his core values and those of his boss, Mayor Mike Bloomberg, transformed a system in a way that exacerbated rather than eradicated inequities. Larry Leverett's leadership of Plainfield, New Jersey, shows how a leader who makes his own values abundantly clear can motivate an entire community to join a movement. I then suggest Marshall Ganz's Public Narrative framework as a model that leaders can use to organize a transformation effort around their values, as Beth Schiavino Narvaez did during her short tenure in Hartford, Connecticut.

THE RULE OF A FEW

The children of NYC have great needs. The city is full of students who are homeless, very poor, or in families struggling to simply earn a decent living. There are also swaths of students from families of hardworking strivers, who could surely be quite successful if given the chance but are in schools with apathetic and unskilled educators. In the early 2000s it was abundantly clear that for too long, NYC schools hadn't been meeting many of those needs, and something had to change. But the election of a new mayor and selection of a new chancellor was a promise that finally, someone was going to do something about the gross inequities in the NYC system and not just tinker around the edges. The simple act of relocating the Department of Education Headquarters to downtown Manhattan, next to City Hall, symbolized the importance of public education to the new mayor. The outrage over too many years of bad results was taking center stage. The New York City schools would have to reckon with its failure to adequately serve one million children each and every year. That's part of why I was so excited to join the administration.

Mayor Mike Bloomberg and Chancellor Joel Klein called their reform agenda "Children First." It was a clever way of signaling that the adults, mainly teachers represented by the powerful United Federation of Teachers (UFT), needed to focus on students rather than themselves. Klein and Bloomberg created a dichotomy between the outrage of those who would champion children above all else, and those whose apathy (real or imagined) had led to generations of poor results. While slogans like "Children First" may be rhetorically compelling, they also disregard those who do the actual work. It suggests that thousands of people are willfully negligent and have the skills, capacity, and resources to meet the needs of all children, yet are just deciding not to. It devalues the people who will actually make the intended change. More than 80 percent of any district's budget is personnel. Adults are doing the daily work of teaching and learning, cleaning, serving, transporting, interacting with families, providing additional services, procuring materials, and managing operations. They are the people who literally make the system work, and through them it gets better, or it doesn't. If they're not inspired by leadership and feel appreciated by those who are calling for a change—even if there is an overwhelmingly compelling reason for it—they won't likely rise to the challenge. They can be threatened by new accountability systems that measure their productivity. They can be controlled and will likely comply. Yet to truly transform a school system, the people who are doing and supporting the actual work of teaching and learning everyday must feel valued and part of the solution.

Klein had dismantled the Microsoft monopoly when he was in the Clinton administration, and he took the same sensibilities to his approach to breaking up the NYC school system. Coupled with Bloomberg's business success, they had a distinct theory of change grounded in two core beliefs about what would spur improvement. The first was to give principals autonomy and hold them accountable for results. The second was to give parents more choice, with the belief that the market would force the closure of poorly performing schools and the expansion of successful ones. These ideas were becoming more popular as the reform era dawned, just as union and teacher bashing were more acceptable, so there was a growing groundswell of support they could ride. But that support was coming from outside forces, including the federal administration, business leaders, and the media, rather than internal stakeholders.

I was a young leader who was both thrilled to be in the thick of a new reform movement and aghast at what I was seeing within Tweed. As one outside consultant said to me, it was, "the greatest mix of ignorance and arrogance" they'd ever seen. After a year in the Office of Programs I became the director of school performance and accountability and was given the opportunity to shape a signature element of the new reform. I learned quickly what I was up against when I sat with Joel's chief of staff and shared some of the research on school accountability. A former hedge fund manager in her mid 40s, she had come to work for the new administration believing that the principles of business that had earned her enormous sums of money could be applied to school improvement. As I presented recent research on accountability system design, she said, "you educators just use the research to make excuses for why Black and

Brown kids aren't learning." Her statement confirmed that my values and beliefs were not in accord with those who were overhauling my home system. And, while there were some positive changes and results that came from the Bloomberg/Klein administration, inequities have been exacerbated throughout the system. In my view, it's an example of how to snatch defeat from the jaws of victory. There's no doubt that they were able to boldly transform a large system quickly around a core set of values and beliefs. They just happened to be the wrong ones, and I can only imagine what would have happened if Bloomberg and Klein had mobilized their considerable resources around what we know actually works to improve public education rather than what we just hope will work based on experience in a different sector.

When I was given the opportunity to become superintendent of Stamford, Connecticut in 2005, two years into my experience at Tweed, I had to think deeply about how I wanted to lead this small city. So, I turned to the model of my mentor, Larry Leverett, who led the Plainfield, New Jersey, public school system for nine years and was the reason I became a superintendent. His values couldn't have been more different from those of Bloomberg and Klein, and they became a beacon for my leadership as I ascended to the top job.

KNOW THYSELF

Larry Leverett's leg was shaking under the table. The stakeholders in the conference room comprising the Leadership Innovation and Change Council (LINCC) couldn't feel it, but sitting next to him I knew that Larry was struggling to maintain the outward calm he projected. He carefully chose his words as he articulated a clear and compelling vision and entreated others to collaborate with him and the team on realizing it. It was 1999, and I was an intern with Larry as part of my doctoral program. Over six months, while attending all cabinet and board meetings and generally being part of the senior staff, I would shadow him for entire days, write memos challenging a decision he made, then work on a project that contributed to the district. For someone who was training to be a superintendent, being an intern and then staying on as director of accountability was a powerful opportunity to apply the knowledge and insight gained in the classroom by learning from a great mentor.

Larry had come to Plainfield in 1995, after a series of leadership positions throughout the state. The school system at the time was about 75 percent Black, 25 percent Latinx, and 80 percent students on free and reduced-priced meals. Larry was looking for a place like Plainfield. He had been fighting for racial and social justice his whole life and knew well the institutional racism facing students that looked like him. His childhood had made Larry a self-described "angry Black man," with a deep sense of passion about how Black children and families are treated in this country. He knew, though, that he had to channel his outrage into a productive force for change, and Plainfield offered just that opportunity. Larry "wanted a broken place, I wanted a context in which a district has a historical record of hardship and great need and children in classrooms and the community that look like me."[3] When Larry took the helm, 25 percent of Plainfield students had met the state benchmark of minimum level of proficiency (MLP) on state tests, which exceeded the standard by 3 percent. This meant that despite the low achievement, the district was not on the state's "bad list." Larry did not anticipate the depth of apathy that educators and the community had about the low achievement. Not being on the state list was a cause for celebration within schools and at the board table. Having 75 percent of the community's students not make MLP barely registered.

Larry knew that he had a deep system transformation effort before him. The question, however, was how to go about it. During his interview process, Larry had given the board a twelve-point framework for change, and by hiring him they accepted his ideas. Thus, he had a mandate, a clear and compelling case, and his internal drive. He could have done what many superintendents do and just started fixing all the problems. That's not an unusual rule that many leaders follow: See a problem, fix the problem. But Larry had a different vision for how the system would change. He wanted to rewrite the rule of who would lead the transformation effort, knowing that for long-lasting change to occur it takes more than the authority of the superintendent. It's easier, in some ways, to pick a fight and charge ahead, up the hill. If you make it to the top, you can claim victory. But if you turn around and there's no one there with you, or too many are struggling to climb, the victory can be fleeting.

Larry also knew that he had to work on himself first. Superintendents are hired for their knowledge, vision, and expertise. They're expected to know what to do and how to do it, and they're charged with leading others to achieve a new result. Superintendents are in the public eye and subject to criticisms from multiple stakeholders. Transparency and vulnerability are risky when sitting in that position. Larry knew that he had the knowledge and skills, and he was driven by his outrage at what he saw in the schools and the apathy in both them and the community. But he also knew his typical modus operandi wouldn't work. At his first gathering of school and system leaders, Larry found them lingering outside as the meeting was about to start and told them to "get your asses inside now." He quickly realized that his outward passion and anger about the low standards of the system wouldn't motivate people to follow him and his vision for kids. It might bring a degree of compliance, but it wouldn't drive the commitment necessary to truly transform the system. Larry needed a new approach to leadership; as he said, "I did a lot of work on myself in Plainfield; I had to move from being an angry black man to think about what's required of an emotionally intelligent leader."[4]

For Larry, emotionally intelligent leadership meant accepting 100 percent of responsibility for problems and listening before acting. It meant ensuring honesty and integrity in his decision-making. I remember asking Larry when I first started working with him why he always sat in the same seat in his office. It was because he had two signs on the wall, one saying "Strong Side," the other "Weak Side." The signs centered him as he did the difficult work of inspiring and leading people to embrace a new standard for themselves and students. Larry's leadership and core values were also driven by his faith. Never one to proselytize, Larry nevertheless was strengthened by Southern Baptist faith tenets, such as being his brother's keeper, minding and harnessing his tongue because you can't take something back once it's spoken; not breaking people's spirit by demeaning them but instead inviting them to join you in the work; and going first to your brother with a problem, and if that doesn't work, seeking counsel. All of these elements of scripture became part of his leadership and sustained his efforts to transform the Plainfield public schools.

COLLECTIVE LEADERSHIP

Larry's outrage, his work on himself, and his faith undergirded his leadership through a commitment to essential core values of emotionally intelligent leadership, equity, collaboration, developing the capacity of others, building relationships, and accountability. Those values became manifest in a new mission for the system, one that became the lifeblood of all of Larry's work to transform teaching and learning throughout the Plainfield public schools. Larry and David Smith, a Plainfield High School student, drafted an elegantly simple statement that would resonate with all stakeholders, including students. I can still repeat it today, as can anyone who worked in Plainfield during those times. "The Plainfield Public Schools, in partnership with its community, will do whatever it takes for all children to reach high academic standards. No alibis. No excuses. No exceptions." In grocery stores, in schools, and at board meeting, people would come up to Larry and throw the mission statement in his face if they felt he wasn't living up to it. Or they avidly repeated it as a way to show solidarity with his agenda. As Larry said, "They held me accountable and I loved it. I wanted to create this sense of buy-in in a simple statement that people could embrace and understand and advocate for and see their roles in partnership with the community. It set a high bar for me, the board and central office and parents and teachers."[5] At the beginning of every meeting the mission statement was recited by all in the room, and posters hung in the wall of every office and school. The mission statement was a clear delineation of Larry's values and a stake in the ground for the work to come.

Larry would have to engage the board, school leaders, teachers, the union, and the community in a long process to overhaul how students were being taught. Before addressing teaching and learning, he chose the "low-hanging fruit" of rallying the community to restore state funds and pass a facilities referendum. Those issues were perfect opportunities for him to make apparent his deep values of social justice, equity, collaboration, and community engagement. Once Larry had some early successes and a clear mission, he harnessed that energy and engagement toward equity and academic achievement. He had hundreds of previously apathetic people in the community and schools ready to follow him. The challenge now was to deeply embed equity-driven transformation throughout the schools. Larry needed teachers to improve their practice, and for that he had to rewrite the rules so that collaboration would get into the DNA of the system. He wanted to break the typical dynamic that exists in too many school districts where negotiations with the teacher's union are tit-for-tats with a focus on step increases, work rules, and benefits. Larry wanted to change how the major players within the system interacted with each other on a daily basis in service of children. It's not enough for a leader to just call out the obvious. They also have to do the deep and complex work of putting new structures and processes in place to get adults to actually change their practice (more on this in Chapter 3). So, everyone was deeply trained in interest-based negotiations, and collaboration was baked into contracts, processes, and regulations.

In Plainfield, LINCC became the hub around which to organize the transformation. LINCC was negotiated into the contract with the Plainfield Education Association so that it became not just a desired approach but a required one for solving problems and addressing challenges. It was where difficult conversations were had and issues were worked through so that the transformation of Plainfield public schools would be a collaborative and unified effort. At the central level the teachers' and administrator's unions had a seat on the council, as did the support staff association, community members, students, and parents. Larry's core values of collaboration and engagement were cemented in policy and administration processes and procedures, giving no quarter to those who wanted to reject the mission and his agenda. After nine years of system transformation that led to clear results, Larry left when board dynamics became overly political and untenable. He rewrote the rules of leadership by working on himself first and gathering others to lead with him, organized around a clear set of values.

SETTING THE STAGE FOR TRANSFORMATION THROUGH STORYTELLING

When I was in graduate school, we studied various urban superintendents to understand how they moved an equity agenda. Our program directors would always return to the idea that you have to know the hill you're going to die on: what's so important to you that you absolutely must see it happen, regardless of the consequences. For me, in Stamford, tracking was my hill. It was a clear equity issue, and I couldn't feel successful as a leader if it wasn't rectified. Yet just decrying the inequity doesn't bring people along. Yes, a leader needs to be firm in their convictions. But they also must invite others to join the movement. By doing so, they not only make their values, beliefs, and intentions clear, they learn the interests of others and can find either common ground or the core of their opposition. Inviting others into authentic conversation isn't always easy. It requires a degree of social-emotional intelligence and self-regulation. One must have the skills to show that they're earnestly seeking authentic perspectives from others. More importantly, collaboration and collective leadership are required to drive an equity agenda. Leaders need followers. They need to know how to activate people in a collective enterprise. They'll find both eager sycophants who want to please the boss and true believers who share their values, and both are necessary to create a movement. But they must also listen to the resistors, who might have real reasons for not joining a movement. Those resistors can become champions of the cause if listened to and engaged. Collaboration doesn't just happen by sitting down at a table. It needs thoughtful processes and rules that bring people together to wrestle with big ideas and small stumbling-blocks. Values are expressed during all of these processes—the hill a leader chooses to climb, their ability to engage with divergent opinions, and their skill at building a movement. In order to collaborate effectively with others, leaders need to be clear about their own values, know those of the community, and bring people together around a shared set of ideas and beliefs about what children need and how to ensure they get it.

Superintendents enter into established systems with distinct contexts and histories. A new superintendent who's trying to push an equity agenda has to figure out how to move the organization and its people toward a collective vision for success between the poles of outrage and apathy. To start this movement, an equity-minded leader needs to be clear about their own values and the hill they're going to die on. They need to know how to self-regulate in order to bring people along. They need to know how to organize collaborative processes that are grounded in collective interests and stakeholder input. They need to build a movement with a "volunteer army" of the willing.[6] The entry and transition processes, and then the creation of a vision and mission, are often the best opportunities to do so. There's nothing radical or innovative about a new superintendent having a one-hundred-day plan that then leads to a strategic planning process with a rewriting of the district's mission and vision statements. In fact, it's expected. An equity-minded leader can use those processes to tease out and make public underlying, long-standing issues, and they can engage different stakeholders than the typical ones. By rewriting these rules, a superintendent can clearly show how they're going to drive an equity agenda.

System leaders are typically hired for their experience and expertise. Their impressive resumes and degrees give them credibility as they make change. Yet they're not always as adept at building relationships with various internal and external communities as they are at analyzing data, managing a spreadsheet, interpreting policy, writing curriculum, or providing professional learning to educators. In schools, educators can connect with families and colleagues through their work and how they take care of children. Central office work and politics are further away from the day-to-day lives of schools, which can make a superintendent's efforts feel that much more removed from the "real" work. White system leaders face an additional challenge. Beyond making their work relevant to educators, schools, families, and communities, they have to show their authentic commitment to an equity agenda. Why should a family or community trust the same people who have oppressed them for so long? Even if a white leader has a great track record of promoting equity and social justice, they have to continually build trust with educators, families and communities of color as they seek transformation.

Often, I've seen white leaders engage with colleagues of color in "oppression Olympics." They detail all the hardships they've experienced, whether it's growing up in a single-parent household or being the first in their family to go to college. They believe that by sharing this with colleagues and families of color, they prove their credibility and their colorblindness. Others, like me, who grew up in a comfortable middle-class suburb with a reasonably stable family may try to prove their authenticity just by listening earnestly and acknowledging the divides. What both of these approaches lack is the need for leaders to make real connections with those they're trying to lead. The white leader who tries to prove that they, too, had it tough disregards centuries of institutional racism and privilege that gave them an inherent advantage. And the silent empath may think they're showing respect for the lived experience of others but fail to build the connection that's necessary to make change. Marshall Ganz's Public Narrative framework can help counteract these dynamics through the creation of a shared story that sets the stage for systems transformation.

Public Narrative can be an effective tool for leaders to move beyond the stale processes of simply developing new language to frame a system's transformation toward actually internalizing shared values that motivate people to do new work. I learned about Ganz's framework during my second superintendency. My prior approach to community engagement, speechmaking, and presentations followed a typical pattern. First, get your audience's attention, then preview the three things you're going to tell them, tell them those three things, summarize, and have a call to action. It generally worked. It kept my public engagements tight and focused. I had once asked Larry how he became such a great public speaker, and he told me "practice." With enough practice I, too, was effective at fulfilling that part of my role. What was missing, however, was an emotional connection to my values, which becomes known through stories. Few could argue with the logic behind a change I was suggesting or an issue I was raising, but I wasn't helping them understand why it was so important to both my personal and our collective values. I wasn't moving our collective story forward. The Public Narrative framework invited the audience to know my story and be part of the collective effort to make a change.

Ganz's Public Narrative framework is elegant in its simplicity. It rests on the stories of Self, Us, and Now. The Story of Self invites others to be in relationship with you. The Story of Us invites them to join your community, and the Story of Now invites them to take action.[7] Superintendents are used to standing before people, dressed in the armor of their suit, and presenting a new initiative. They're used to getting press coverage, being asked tough questions from stakeholders and board members, and having watchdogs and citizen journalists post inaccurate information. The scrutiny they endure can cause them to can hide behind PowerPoint slides as they propose a change. This is a familiar exercise, to differing degrees and effect, within many school systems. What can be missing is the invitation to join a movement, one based on shared values. And when leaders, particularly white ones, are trying to lead an equity agenda, the status quo is not sufficient.

Most superintendents present the board with a "first one hundred days" plan, often as part of the interview process. This is an opportunity for the superintendent to get to know the community and become known to internal and external stakeholders. Typically, the new superintendent will write a public letter about what they'll do during those hundred days: lots of meetings with important people, school visits, media interviews, and document reviews, and then a public presentation of what they've learned. Entry, when done right, can be a great way for stakeholders to get to know the new leader and their core values through their story.[8] Entry is a standard rule for system leaders to follow. However, rather than have it be focused on the typical issues facing the system, leaders should use it as an opportunity to tell their story. By doing so, they make their values known to a wider public. Stakeholders already have perceptions and beliefs based on their experiences. While a new leader will have to share their impressions of the system, what people really want is to get to know who the leader is, what motivates them, and why they should be trusted. Ganz's Story of Self is where a new superintendent can inspire followers to become part of the volunteer army through sharing their values.

Transition is different from entry as it's about the entire organization, not just the leader. System transformation efforts are about transitioning from one state of being into another. William Bridges' book *Managing Transitions*[9] is the best guide for new leaders to use as they help internal and external communities embrace what a transformed organization can look like. As transition is a collective enterprise with stakeholders having different ideas about what should change and when, if at all, leaders need to bring in multiple voices to determine both what needs to change and when. Some people have been outraged and demand change immediately; others are apathetic and may not even know the state of things. The school board is further ahead than the rest of the community, as they've been interviewing candidates and getting ready to work with a new superintendent for months prior to the actual change in leadership. The outraged will have their list of demands, the apathetic will nod politely in agreement and then go back to doing what they've always done, and the resistors will find ways to challenge a new leader. A thoughtful and deliberate approach to engaging all of these stakeholders will at least neutralize resistance and at best initiate a volunteer army.

In order to address long-standing issues within the system that have kept some students from achieving success, school systems have to do something fundamentally different. Tinkering around the edges won't work if there's a moral imperative to ensure that all students have access to high-quality instruction. Whether it's adopting new curriculum, making personnel changes, requiring professional learning, opening up advanced courses, or engaging families and students differently, an equity-based strategy requires a fundamental reconsideration of the entire state of the organization. A leader is thus obligated to have a thoughtful approach to this transition. The best transition processes are ones where a mix of stakeholders and outside experts analyze the conditions of the district through interviews, focus groups, data analyses, and document reviews. This process helps tell the Story of Us; what the current condition is of the system and its needs, challenges, and opportunities. It also sets up the mission and vision setting process, which is the Story of Now.

There's a standard rule in every school district in America to have a vision and mission statement. These statements attempt to inspire employees and the community to embrace twenty-first-century skills, the achievement of every student, college and career readiness, self-actualization, and service to the community. Often written by committee with every word debated, most of them look the same throughout the nation. Smart leaders, however, can use the process of developing a mission and vision to put the emphasis on the values needed to lay the groundwork for powerful equity work. They can rewrite the rules by using it as an opportunity for deep engagement and to lay the foundation for transformation based on shared values. Any organization, including schools and school districts, needs a compelling vision and mission to both ground the work of its people and communicate an aspiration. It's a standard rule of public education that at worst is ignored by employees and the public, and at best is a stake in the ground for transformation. Equity-minded system leaders can use it as an opportunity for the latter through the process of crafting it and by making it the framework and criteria for decision-making.

Developing mission and vision statements typically entails one of two standard processes, often with guidance from an outside consultant. Sometimes the board starts the process and establishes its core values and may even write vision and mission statements, which then ignites a strategic planning process for staff and the community. Or, vice versa, the staff and community engage in a process to develop new vision and mission statements, which then leads to staff developing a new strategic plan with board approval. These processes can be a balancing act for system leaders, especially superintendents. They have to allow the board and/or the community to lead, yet still influence the outcome. After all, one of the board's main roles is to establish a mission and vision for the chief executive to organize around. Moreover, true transformation in public school systems happens with the board and community, not in spite of them, so a superintendent can't be too far ahead of where they both are. The superintendent is the steward of the community's values. Miles's law rings true: Where you stand is where you sit. Superintendents' orientations and allegiances are often toward those who hire them, which is necessary for survival but is not the basis for transformation. Their success comes from those who they lead and who are affected by change. Without their support, a leader stands little chance of making transformational change. A leader's values are the fulcrum of this seesaw between those who want to perpetuate the status quo and those who clamor for change. An equity lens and a social justice stance requires that leaders have nonnegotiable values that encompass the entirety of the system and the complexity of the change process, and that they can inspire others to join a leader in their transformation efforts.

PUTTING THE GANZ NARRATIVE TO WORK IN HARTFORD

When I became superintendent of schools in Montgomery County, Maryland, I needed a trusted right-hand person to help me transform the system. This person would need to know teaching and learning, be able to lead principals and principal supervisors, and be deeply grounded in equity. I immediately reached out to Beth Schiavino Narvaez. Beth had interned with me when I was in Stamford, so I knew her well. She had been a successful principal in a depressed district and after her internship with me became chief academic officer in Springfield, Massachusetts. After working in Montgomery County Public Schools (MCPS) with me for a few years, establishing new systems for coaching, support, and intervention across our 202 schools, Beth got the opportunity to become superintendent of Hartford, Connecticut. When I asked her why she wanted the job, she told me that she not only trained for it, but too many women were stuck in the number two slot and didn't ascend to the top. So, when Hartford called, she picked up the phone.

Hartford is the capital city of Connecticut. Like most urban areas in the state, it's been neglected for many years, and a significant number of its one-hundred and twenty-two thousand citizens are in poverty. Of the twenty thousand students enrolled in Hartford schools, about 15 percent are white from surrounding suburbs, with most of the Hartford students being Black or Latinx. The district meets the federal threshold for all students to receive free meals, even though many students in magnet schools don't qualify. Hartford's forty-eight schools have been subject to a court case known as *Sheff v. O'Neill*, first brought in 1989 and settled in 2003. Essentially, Sheff established interdistrict school desegregation among Hartford and its neighbors through the establishment of magnet schools. White students from the suburbs are offered seats in urban magnet schools, which then creates very diverse student populations within well-staffed, beautiful new buildings. Schools have distinct themes and innovative instructional programs, such as the environmental science magnet school with its own butterfly conservatory. Hartford students who don't get their name called in the lottery are left to their neighborhood schools. These schools have far fewer resources, and the highly needy population, many of them English language learners and students with special needs, are left to learn the basic curriculum, many in run-down buildings waiting to be renovated by the state. Student achievement falls along predictable lines: magnet school students perform at high levels on state tests, neighborhood school students don't.

Beth knew that she had a challenge before her as she entered her first superintendency. An unassuming young white woman taking the helm of a complex district of mostly Black and Latinx students and families would have a difficult time anywhere. Hartford's clear inequities and its status as the capital city, which brought increased media scrutiny, made the challenge that much greater. But Beth knew the work. She had succeeded at every level of a school system, had been trained by experts, and had implemented innovative change efforts that led to real results. Beth knew the work ahead was complex, difficult, and political. Yet she wasn't fully aware of the challenge of going from the number two slot to the number one. When you're in a superintendent's cabinet you interact with the community, families, and the board, but you always have the top person to fall back on. When you're the end of the line, the necessary leadership capacities are different. She had to learn a new way of leading that invited people to follow her. That's when Beth turned to Marshall Ganz's work.

Beth brought together outside experts and internal stakeholders to help her determine the pressing issues facing Hartford. And they were many. The crux of the issue in Hartford is the vestiges of the *Sheff* decision. Magnet schools remained great places for diverse groups of kids to learn, although even there, problems were arising, as the surrounding suburbs had become more diverse and not enough white kids were enrolling, which then decreased available seats for Hartford students. Neighborhood schools were the polar opposite, with the most vulnerable students being educated in the lowest-resourced schools. Anyone in Hartford who had been paying attention knew that there were gross inequities among the schools. No one, however, had brought people together to transparently look at the facts. When they begin a new position, leaders have to choose how much information they want to put into the public domain, because once it's out there, you're responsible; if you name it, you claim it. Beth, though, had always been about transparent, collective leadership grounded in the data. If the data were clear, they needed to be talked about by the entire community, and the variability between magnet and neighborhood schools could not have been more stark.

The other major concern for Beth, and one that was at the core of her being as an educator, was the lack of focus on teaching and learning. Beth's entire career had been about instructional leadership, and she was deeply committed to an equity agenda rooted in high expectations for both students and adults. Beth had started her teaching career in a small city where the ineq-uities among children and communities in our country were apparent. As she began her leadership journey, NCLB was making it abundantly clear that public schools were failing too many students. She was fortunate to be men-tored by a principal who taught her that excellence and equity were possible, and, in fact, the most important job of a school leader. When she became a principal, Beth was prepared to lead her team in a collective effort to improve teaching and learning for every child. Those values—high expectations, col-lective leadership, focus on teaching and learning, data matters, and invest in people—grounded her superintendency and her urgency to focus on teach-ing and learning in Hartford.

Once the transition report was completed, it clearly laid out the Story of Us for all stakeholders. The facts on the ground were incontrovertible. Beth took the report out on the road and shared it with multiple commu-nity groups. Although she was still learning to fulfill the public role of a superintendent, Beth was effective at getting the schools and community to coalesce around the realities and the potential of Hartford. The urgent question before them became one of what to do about the gross inequities. Resources had diminished, enrollment in schools was declining, and hard choices had to be made. The election of a new mayor who offered her luke-warm support portended political difficulties, as the mayor appointed five of the nine board members. But the status of the district demanded action, and that's what Beth was there to do.

Beth and her team used the transition plan to create the Story of Now by launching a strategic planning process. Through extensive community engagement Beth and her chief of staff developed a new vision for Hartford schools grounded in the "four E's": expectations, engagement, expanded capacity, and equity. These reflected her core values, developed over years, and served as a theory of action. *If we have high expectations for students and adults, and if we engage stakeholders, and if we expand the capacity of adults to serve children, then we will achieve equity.*[10] She set the goal of 100 percent college acceptance for every Hartford student, which reflected her belief that if it was expected of suburban students who came to Hartford magnet schools, it was good for Hartford students too. Beth also lever-aged the innovations that she saw in many schools and expanded them to the whole district. For example, they partnered magnet and neighborhood high schools as "high school centers of innovation" around mastery-based, blended, and project-based learning, including a robust internship program. Beth also established a core literacy program for elementary schools. Her focus on developing the capacity of adults manifested in a comprehensive leadership development program and an investment in professional learning for teachers.

Despite the energy and excitement of a new vision grounded in the Story of Now, endemic problems plagued her and the schools. Twenty-five percent of students were chronically absent, so they brought in "City Connects," an initiative started by Mary Lynch in Boston College to ensure that they knew where every student was and could get them the services and support they needed to get back to school. Declining resources were becoming a significant barrier to achieving her goals, and it was clear that staff would have to be cut and schools would have to be closed. As Beth and her team began working on these difficult issues, the mayor's lack of support became more pronounced, and Beth could see the writing on the wall. It became easy to blame her for long-standing issues in the system, despite her short tenure, and it was apparent that making the necessary structural changes in order to right-size it would be a massive fight that she would most likely lose. Following the rule that a leader should "get out before they push you out," Beth was offered an opportunity to pursue another position that would better serve her and her family, so she jumped at it, leaving the next superintendent, a Hartford native, to execute on her plans.

CONCLUSION

To successfully transform school systems in a lasting way, leaders must make their values known and unify a community around a set of shared ones. And they must also measure the extent to which their actions and those of others are aligned with those values. Through surveys, document reviews, and focus groups, system leaders can understand whether or not a change happened in accordance with the espoused value. For example, if collaboration is a stated shared value, yet a principal decided to make a significant change to the schedule without consulting teachers and parents, the value was not adhered to. That principal's supervisor can review the decision-making process as part of their evaluation of the principal and can even get input from teachers and parents. If equity is a value of the board and community, where does it show up in resource allocation decisions? Focus groups with students, employees, and families can give a system leader insight into whether the system is respecting and valuing their voices as decisions are made. No single measure will tell a leader everything they need to know about whether a value was adhered to, but by asking the right questions of enough people, they can get a sense of whether the system is acting in accordance with the stated values.

In smaller districts leaders have to consider whether their values are a match with those of the board of education and the internal and external communities. In broken systems new leaders aren't brought in to maintain the status quo, but the tractor beam of local context is powerful. Even with a clear mandate and compelling evidence that change is needed, new leaders have to find the balance between their sense of urgency and that of both the board that hired them, and the values and beliefs of the people they're going to lead in the transformation effort. There's a constant "push–pull" dynamic where new system leaders both get behind their employees and communities and help push them to the top of the mountain while simultaneously pulling others along with them. And some will stay at the bottom and never ascend. When a leader is clear with stakeholders about their own values and story, they can find the common ground upon which to lay the foundation for a transformation effort. Going about doing so, however, is a delicate and intricate dance.

The Bloomberg/Klein administration radically overhauled the NYC schools according to their clear values that school systems should be run like a business. In doing so, they at least proved that a massive and entrenched bureaucracy can be transformed, regardless of whether the underpinnings of the change are the right ones. They led with their values without getting enough people to follow, which is not a recipe for lasting change. Larry Leverett spent nine years working with the community, building relationships, and forcefully advocating for equity and social justice on behalf of Plainfield's children. Subsequent superintendents haven't been as strong or as smart, but the system hasn't retrenched to the broken state it was in prior to Larry's arrival. Beth Schiavino Narvaez's tenure was cut short in Hartford, but she showed that a thoughtful and deliberate approach to engaging the community, putting the facts on the table in a transparent way, and building a collective narrative about the future could begin a transformation effort that her successor has implemented. There is no singular approach to organizing a transformation effort. Yet a leader still has to make their values clear and ensure that those who they seek to bring along in the transformation effort share their beliefs about what's possible.

3

Who Gets to Make What Kind of Decision

THE SUPERINTENDENCY COMES with a lot of power. The top leader gets to rally stakeholders around a vision. They present a budget for the board and local funding authority to approve. They can establish a culture through modelling behaviors and involving different constituents. They can implement initiatives intended to increase achievement or address long-standing issues. They can highlight inequities in the system and spur their team to address them. They can reorganize their central offices around a clear set of goals. Yet, in most districts, the only decision a superintendent gets to make all alone is when they have to call a snow day. Every other decision requires adherence to formal rules and regulations, implicit and explicit expectations (also known as past practice), and politics.

Early in my tenure as chief executive officer of PDK International, I worked with my team to write a grant proposal to expand our work. After we drafted it, I turned to my colleagues and asked, "Does this need to be approved by anyone?" I had never worked outside of a public-school system and had no idea that in the nonprofit and private sectors, you can take action without having to consult a variety of stakeholders. Sure, I have a board of directors, but they have no interest in my day-to-day actions; they just want results. My team looked at me askance and quite nicely said to their new boss, "Uh, no." That's when the guardrails that contain and constrain the superintendency became so clear to me.

To make a substantive change within a school system can take months of planning, engagement, review, and modification before it gets to the board table for a vote. And then resources need to be allocated to support the initiative. Some of this is essential, as rules around expenditures and personnel can control for malfeasance and corruption. Moreover, public school systems, after all, are engines of democracy, and the public should have a say in how the system operates. Yet, the guardrails that keep the system honest and allow for engagement can also thwart innovation and the swift action needed to address entrenched problems. More problematically, they can water down and hold up efforts to address inequities. In fact, they're almost designed to do so.

This chapter is about rewriting the rules of decision-making. From formal governance structures to school improvement planning, I will share how leaders who organize an equity agenda can establish clarity and cohesion about who gets to make what kinds of decisions and why. Public education systems are designed to perpetuate the status quo, and decision-making processes are its ultimate manifestation. Leaders who seek to transform the status quo so that the needs of the most vulnerable are met must, then, consider how decisions are made. A change will last only as long as the superintendent's contract if it's not baked into the system, and decision-making processes are an essential part of that recipe.

INTEGRITY IN DECISION-MAKING PROCESSES

A superintendent seeking to transform a system around an equity agenda will face criticism and pushback. Not only are there a myriad of difficult decisions, there are some people, usually white parents, who are threatened by them. Their privilege and entitlement are on the table when a leader is trying to level the playing field. Take the issue of opening access to advanced courses in high school. This is a clear equity issue, and even the U.S. Office of Civil Rights publishes data on whether a district's Advanced Placement and gifted classes represent the demographics of the district as a whole. There is no educational reason to limit access to advanced coursework, yet districts do it all the time. While the logic and reasoning for taking such an action may be unimpeachable, a leader who wants to open up that access must ensure that the decision-making process has integrity, as that is what is likely to be challenged.

An equity initiative such as opening access to advanced courses challenges the very foundations of many of our public-school systems. The American ethos is to treasure something if I have it and you don't, regardless of its intrinsic value. Access to advanced courses has been one method for keeping white people happy in diverse districts. By providing them with a special designation of "gifted and talented" or allowing them to take high school math in middle school, and then stuffing their schedules with Honors and Advanced Placement (AP) courses in high school, leaders of diverse districts attend to the entitlement and privilege of many white people. This privilege is exercised in a myriad of ways. Many white people are not shy about stating that they're doing the public school system a favor by staying in the schools rather than moving to a neighboring town or going to private school. They join the PTA to ensure the principal knows their interests, and they wield influence through fund-raising and positions on committees. They're more likely to be involved in local politics, sometimes by supporting and raising money for elected officials. They're more likely to have the means and comfort to take time to attend board meetings and speak about an initiative. They have access to information and expertise through professional networks and the time to then post it on citizen watchdog blogs, listservs, and Facebook. None of these exercises in power and privilege are formal parts of the decision-making process within a school system. But they create an environment that a superintendent will have to navigate when pushing an equity agenda.

Let's consider all of the steps that have to be taken to open access. Under the best of circumstances, it's difficult. First, policies and regulations have to be reviewed and possibly revised, as those may delineate student eligibility. The board will want to know the perspectives of parents and teachers, as well as the evidence to support this decision. Then they'll need to understand associated costs, as they're always weighing the return on investments, and if they choose to do this, they may not be able to do something else. Throughout deliberations, they'll be lobbied by constituents on both sides, while teacher associations may challenge the new work required to help kids succeed in advanced courses. This decision is political, as different interests need to be arbitrated, just so that regulations and policies can be changed.

Even if the board is supportive, a superintendent must ensure that their senior leadership team is on board. When Brian Osborne was deleveling middle school math, he found that the district math supervisor wasn't supportive. She was working with schools to create microlevels of students among classes so that even though courses were no longer designated as advanced or not, the assignment of students within courses followed the old patterns of segregating students by perceived abilities. There are formal written policies, regulations, contracts, and procedures within schools and districts, and then there are past practices and workarounds that can maintain the status quo. Multiple central office departments must change some of their practices to ensure the success of opening access. The curriculum department will have to consider changes to both content and pedagogy so that teachers have multiple ways of engaging students in rich content. Teachers will need professional development to understand how to support students they may not have typically taught. The data team will need to determine the right algorithms to identify and assign students according to new rules. If the district has an equity department, their role as either monitors, supporters, and/or implementers will need to be determined. Students may require additional supports in order to succeed, especially if they're current or former English language learners or have an Individual Education Plan (IEP) or 504 plan. The human resources department may need to help schools ensure that they're assigning talent to task. Finally, the principal supervisors must support and hold principals accountable for doing this new work. All along the way, there are decisions that have to be made and landmines that can blow the initiative up if not swept for.

At the school level, in order to successfully open access, principals will have to be coached, supported, and held accountable. They not only have to get their staff to embrace the initiative, they have to make sure it succeeds. And they can undermine it at any time. Principals need to be well-versed in the new regulations, policies, and procedures. They have to carve out time for professional learning and work with their leadership teams to create new schedules. New mechanisms for supporting students have to be put in place, and the most effective teachers need to be assigned to the students who need them the most. Above all, the principal has to rally their teachers, support professionals, students, and parents to embrace the idea. They have to carry the flag of equity and actually implement the new work. And they are the first line of defense when the criticism begins.

How, then, should a leader who's trying to transform a system through an equity lens approach decision-making within this complex environment? In my view, integrity of the process is key. It is expected that not everyone is going to agree with every decision a leader makes. However, people have to trust that the leader made the decision by using the most comprehensive information available and considering multiple perspectives. Moreover, stakeholders have the right to know the data and information that were used, who was involved in making the decision, the opportunities for stakeholder participation, and the timeline for implementation. That's integrity in decision-making.

Two purposes are served when there is integrity in decision-making. The first, and most important, is that it will likely lead to a better decision by taking into account multiple points of view. The more diverse a system is, and the more it needs to change, the more likely there will be different ideas about how to help students. Not all of these perspectives are valid, fact-based, or even relevant, and some people with a particular bone to pick will see every issue through the lens of their grievance. But most stakeholders have honest and valid questions, concerns, and ideas about their schools. The resistors, in particular, can help a leader understand the barriers they will face when trying to push forward a new initiative. Too often that resistance is dismissed as being against the interests of children or too concerned with adult issues. And sometimes it is. A decision-making process with integrity, however, can mitigate against these dynamics and separate the wheat from the chaff. When enough people and perspectives inform the decision, a leader is able to determine the legitimacy of the input. After all, research methodology is based on sample size; the bigger the sample the more valid the data. Gathering input when making decisions can be like conducting research.

The second purpose for having integrity in decision-making is political. Transparent processes engender trust. They can be more complicated and riskier, but when people can see how something is done, they're more likely to support it or, at the very least, begrudgingly accept it. The resistors have a hard time pushing back if they were involved and their issues were addressed. This then means that leaders must be absolutely clear about how and whether issues that were raised were considered within the final decision. The folks who tend to stay on the sidelines need the decision to pass the "smell test." When they do decide to pay attention, perhaps from having heard about the new initiative on the soccer field, after church, at a cocktail party, or from reading it in the newspaper, does it make sense? Does it seem to be pretty reasonable? Of course, all of the information about the decision will be made through the filter of the reporter, the friend, or the Facebook post. Yet, the more transparent the leader is about how the decision is made, the more likely it is to pass the "smell test" with the silent majority.

The more complicated political dynamic is with elected officials and employee associations. They have actual formal authority when it comes to decision-making, which is why superintendents spend so much time attending to their needs, whims, and demands. A Board of Education can simply vote no; an employee association can bargain the contractual elements, threaten a strike, or hold a vote of no confidence; a funding authority can refuse to allocate the resources. When a decision-making process has integrity, however, a leader can reduce the likelihood of any of that occurring. By being upfront and transparent in the beginning about how the decision will be made, getting agreement from the above entities about their own roles, and then following through, an equity initiative stands a better chance of succeeding.

NEW RULES OF DECISION-MAKING

To approach decision-making in new ways that promote integrity, there are four areas that superintendents need to attend to, each of which will be delineated in the following sections. The first is the board of education, which holds the most power in a school system. Through John Carver's Policy Governance, a superintendent can establish appropriate lines of authority, management, and accountability. Second, by attending to principal supervision, system leaders can promote central office alignment. Third, an interest-based approach to negotiations can increase collaboration. Fourth, a "loose–tight" approach to school improvement planning can help schools improve their practice to better meet the needs of their students.

Policy Governance

Superintendents spend an inordinate amount of time on the "care and feeding" of their boards. According to the 2020 American Association of School Administrators (AASA) decennial poll of the superintendency, a substantial amount of their time is spent managing their boards.[1] Get a superintendent alone, perhaps with a drink at a conference, out of earshot of constituents, and you can guarantee that they'll bemoan the gyrations that board members regularly put them through. There are countless examples of boards that have driven a superintendent out over petty disagreements and board members that ask for special favors from senior staff. Over ten years as superintendent, I worked for approximately fifty different board members. Some were professionals who clearly understood their role as stewards of the system. Some were long-time activists who just wanted to make the system better. And some were, frankly, shameful in pursuing their own agendas by settling vendettas from when they worked in the system or being solely interested in serving their own entitled constituents.

Boards of Education are distinctly political entities. Members get elected by advocating for or against an issue and often represent a distinct geographic area and constituency. They may promise to hold the chief executive accountable or bring certain voices to the table. They argue for transparency, better communication, and results. Sometimes board members are single-issue candidates who seek to influence the outcome of one distinct issue or are directly tied to an interest group. A school board position can also be a stepping-stone for higher political office, which means a member with aspirations may seek media attention and an association with distinct groups or positions if it helps them in the future.

Boards of Education have enormous formal power in the system, with their three main roles being hiring and evaluating the superintendent, setting policy, and passing a budget. Yet regular committee and full meetings consist of numerous items not related to those main roles. And that's where equity issues often come to the fore. Boards approve personnel decisions, with some even having power over hiring teachers. They approve curriculum revisions and adoptions. They approve transportation routes, the siting of new schools, and the renovations of old ones. Boards approve policies that dictate the work of schools, such as grading and reporting and assignment of students to special programs. Some boards not only approve contracts with employee bargaining units, they sit on the negotiating teams. Boards not only oversee the district's strategic plan, they may review and approve school improvement plans.

Board members also have significant informal power. They have relationships in the system that can be used to gather information and sow discontent. They can call meetings and request additional information and further analysis in order to slow down initiatives. I've seen board members go to individual principals and central office leaders and demand they take action on a particular issue. Board members can insist that certain community members get face time with the superintendent or that they attend a particular community meeting at night.

A superintendent seeking to transform the system through an equity lens has to manage all of these formal and informal powers of the board. They need board members to feel that they are appropriately exercising their authority and having their interests met, while not compromising the integrity of the decision-making process. Boards can be powerful allies in pushing an equity agenda through and, in fact, are the keys to the success of any new agenda. They can serve an important role as the voice of the community and as a check and balance on the superintendent and their team. At their best, they can engage other elected officials in order to garner support, and they can use their community ties to work with stakeholders. When I was in Stamford, the boards during my first three years paved the way for our detracking work. I simply could not have done it without them, as they were clear that they wanted it and were willing to risk their positions to block and tackle so that I could move the system forward.

While boards can be allies for an equity agenda, they can also thwart one. School systems need an approach that keeps them focused on their work while allowing for the superintendent to focus on theirs. John Carver's Policy Governance, in my mind, is the best strategy for keeping everyone focused on their appropriate work while allowing for swift and bold action to address long-standing equity issues. The traditional rules for managing board members can be rewritten to manage processes and results through policy governance.

Every school system has a policy manual that guides decision-making. Many policies are compulsory and follow state guidelines; others reflect the local context, and some follow the whims of a particular board at a particular time. Policies have regulations that guide the actions of central office and school leaders as they purchase equipment and supplies, hire staff (a process also bound by contracts), or select materials to support curriculum units. Frankly, most policies go unnoticed by both board members and system leaders most of the time—until, that is, there's a reason to use policy as a mechanism to thwart or accelerate progress.

School boards can bog an initiative down in policy discussions if they so choose. Equity agendas and their corresponding controversy can be compromised if the system's policies aren't aligned or are ambiguous. For example, a student assignment policy may allow for open access to advanced courses by either being silent about the issue, clearly stating that philosophy, or leaving it to regulations. Or, such a policy can delineate the qualifications for taking an advanced course. A leader who seeks to open access to advanced courses will have to consider the policy landscape as they do so. Some policy decisions fly under the radar and get little public attention. Others, especially those grounded in equity, are more likely to provoke some stakeholders to lobby board members, speak publicly, and organize either for or against a change. This process can take months or even years. Transforming how a system works in order to serve more students at a higher level can get bogged down for too long in the politics of changing policies, which only benefits those who seek to maintain the status quo.

John Carver's Policy Governance is an approach that I have seen work well, albeit too infrequently, when trying to keep a board "above the line."[2] Above the line is board work; below is staff work. Above is governance, below is management. The board and superintendent may have an annual retreat where they determine processes to stay in their appropriate roles and make promises to do so. But it's hard to build into their ongoing, day-to-day work. Too often, the determination of what's above and what's below the line happens after the fact. Boards as a whole don't usually go below the line; it's individual board members that typically transgress. That then leads the superintendent and perhaps board leaders to retrospectively address the violation. Policy governance creates the operating system for both the board and the chief executive to fulfill their appropriate roles more proactively, transparently, and efficiently.

This chapter doesn't allow for a full description of Carver's model. His book *Boards that Make a Difference* is the bible for any leader seeking to learn more about his framework. When I was in Stamford, we began to implement parts of his model, which showed that you don't have to rework everything to start operating differently. Essentially, there are four main components: ends, executive limitations, board management delegation, and governance process. Ends are results. They're about the values of the organization, what it stands for, and what it expects to achieve. In an equity agenda, the ends are that each and every child have access to high-quality instruction and necessary supports that prepare them to leave school with more options than they came in. Executive limitations are the boundaries and guidelines that staff must work within to achieve the end. They are the means that ensure ethical actions to achieve the results. Board management delegation delineates the process by which the board gives staff authority to act within the limitations to achieve the ends. And governance process is focused on the work of the board itself to ensure that it is staying "above the line."

The real work of policy governance, in my experience, is the structured process that the board and chief executive engage in when working on complex, difficult issues such as an equity agenda. It requires that both parties slow down inquiry to speed up action by ensuring absolute clarity of expectations. Part of this process is what Carver calls "reasonable interpretation." Essentially, this means that the CEO/superintendent repeats to the board the relevant section of policy they're attending to, interprets the meaning of the section so that there's agreement on all sides that it's reasonable, and then cites data to verify the interpretation. By laying this all out upfront, the board and superintendent then avoid the "gotcha" games and ambiguity that all too-often sink an equity agenda.

Let's use the example of opening access to advanced courses to further understand how a leader can use policy governance. Suppose that after a visioning process the board clearly states that it values equity and that all students should have access to high-quality teaching and learning, with necessary supports, that prepare them for college and careers; this is their ends. The board and superintendent would then sit down and determine how far the chief executive can go within the current policies, with student assignment being the key policy lever. The superintendent determines that, in fact, some students, mostly Black and Latinx, don't take upper-level classes that prepare students for post-secondary success. The means by which the Board's values will be enacted, and the ends achieved, is through opening access, and the executive is limited to this action. The board delegates to management the authority to work with the principals to open access and creates a monitoring calendar and agreed-upon set of data to determine the effectiveness of this move. The board also ensures that its committee structure, meeting agendas, public reporting, and monitoring processes allow the superintendent to enact what they agreed upon, which is the governance process.

It's never, of course, quite as simple as this, and there are many other aspects of policy governance that can help a superintendent and board transform a system. In my own experience, I learned that despite public and private agreements to implement a new approach to shared governance, individual board members can, in the end, do what they want. Policy governance, however, creates a transparent decision-making framework for leaders to work within. Expectations of both parties and the public can then be managed, and integrity is increased. Policy governance is no panacea when it comes to decision-making, but it can be used to construct a playing field for leaders to work within when making very complex changes to public school systems.

The Role of the Central Office in Decision-Making

The modern school system central office is a recent phenomenon. Until the advent of the standards and accountability era, system leaders were focused on operations while schools handled instruction. Now, central office staff lead professional learning, write curriculum, and implement and monitor programs, along with allocating resources, analyzing data, hiring staff, supervising principals, and engaging the community. Some of these functions may be necessary; others can be pushed back to schools. Regardless, a myriad of decisions made in the central office directly impact schools and can hinder or accelerate an equity agenda and the superintendent's ability to transform a system. The rule that needs to be rewritten is the command-and-control stance that many central offices have toward school improvement. The way to rewrite this rule is by focusing on how principals are supervised and supported, which, in its purest form, is the essential work of central office.

System leaders serve the needs of two masters. One is the students and families within a community. I always tell new superintendents and central office leaders that a school community is going to be there a lot longer than you are, and its context and culture must be attended to when pushing change. The other serves external entities, whether it's the board, the local funding authority, or the state. A central office leader's success rests on their ability to help schools improve student achievement without directly working with students or supervising teachers. And therein lies the rub. Schools may have their own ideas about how to improve student achievement, while the central office wants consistency among schools to make resource allocation and monitoring more efficient. Central office leaders are under pressure to quickly meet the standards set by the board and the state. They also have the means to get the board to allocate monies toward a distinct initiative and the platform to sell that approach to the community. They're charged with monitoring and reporting on results, especially for vulnerable populations such as SWDs, ELLs, and students eligible for free and reduced priced lunch. They have to interpret state regulations for schools and monitor and report progress to meet accountability requirements. Given this work of central offices, it's no wonder they take a command-and-control stance, as it's easier and more efficient to manage. These dynamics, coupled with a high degree of pressure for results, can lead to distrust between schools and central office.

The makeup of the actual personnel who staff central office can also stymie transformation efforts through a top-down approach. There are typically three kinds of people who work in central office. One is the successful principal who gets tapped to lead an office based on their ability to move a school. They're expected to bring their expertise to bear on a larger number of schools, and often they have aspirations to become a superintendent. Another is the staffer who has found a good home in the world of program administration, professional learning, curriculum development, or some other area and enjoys the work of serving schools. Yet another type is the person who was placed there due to poor performance at a school and can't be removed from the system due to contractual and legal strictures. Each of these types feed the beast of command and control. The expert may think that others should do it like they did, given their own success. The administrator finds it easier if everyone is doing things the same way. And the disgraced doesn't have the knowledge, skill, or credibility to do much more than fulfill the basic obligations of central office administration.

Given all of this, how should an equity-minded superintendent lead their central office staff? To my mind, the first problem to be solved is to determine the appropriate unit of change, which is the principal. One of the greatest challenges with central office functionality is the different constituents each department serves. By design, central offices serve distinct groups within schools and report to the state on discrete components of the school. Take, for example, special populations of SWDs and ELLs. They each have complex funding, assessment, monitoring, and accountability rules that bind their instructional programs. The central office administrator is in charge of making sure every "I" is dotted and every "T" is crossed. Their performance is based on whether teachers and principals who serve these populations are in compliance, and whether their students make progress. Yet, ELL and SWD students are in classes and schools with other students, some of whom may make the school eligible for Title 1 dollars, which is a whole different accountability and regulatory scheme. For the special program administrator, who is their unit of change? Is it the teacher who works directly with the classified student, is it the assistant principal in charge of those areas within the school, or is it the principal who has overall authority over the school? Too often, program administrators focus on the first, when I believe it is the principal who should be the sole unit of change for central office administrators.

PRINCIPAL AS THE UNIT OF CHANGE

There are no great schools without great principals. I've seen good schools without a great principal, typically ones with a stable set of teachers and few vulnerable students. But for a school that serves students with great needs and requires an equity agenda, a great principal must be at the helm. Great principals don't always find much value or credibility in the central office. After all, they're not only accountable for what goes on day to day and for annual results, they know their school better than anyone. How, then, should a system leader find the right "loose–tight" balance between ensuring that a principal adheres to the district's vision for children and leads their faculty, staff, and community toward success? The answer lies in organizing for adult learning around the primacy of principal supervision.

The best leaders lead their own learning,[3] which means that system leaders need to help principals be active learners within their communities. Whether the district is large, mid-size, or small, system leaders need to see the development of instructional leadership as their most important role. Since adults learn best when they're trying to solve a real problem of practice through collaboration and guided practice, principal supervision is about helping leaders learn. Everything else in central office is secondary. System leaders must first increase efficiencies so that principals aren't overburdened by the operational aspects of their job, such as hiring staff and procuring supplies. I don't want to underestimate the challenge of doing this, but it is necessary when trying to improve principal supervision. Then, principal supervisors need to work with other central staff to determine the instructional priorities of the system and who will be providing what new learning to whom, and when. Too often this exercise is a competition among different departments who are all jockeying for teachers' time. The superintendent has the responsibility to insist that central office staff support schools in a coordinated fashion rather than in the typical discrete events that they're used to. Then attention can be turned to the development of instructional leadership.

If a superintendent has put in place clear, nonnegotiable equity goals, they must then support the process by which school leaders realize those goals. Again, one way that is all too common is to simply demand that every school do the same thing and then measure the fidelity of implementation. Such a high-modernist[4] approach can get quick results, especially if the system is broken and needs a quick fix. Yet it won't engender the kind of transformation schools truly need to sustain long-term changes in adult practice that lead to greater learning for all students. That work can only be done by a school community that embraces the challenge of equity and their own learning. Principals must lead that learning, and they must be learners themselves. System leaders must then guide, support, and coach principals individually and within communities of practice, so that they can improve their skills as instructional leaders.

Decision-making, then, within this paradigm is evident through principal supervision and school improvement planning processes. It is essential that the superintendent be absolutely clear on the nonnegotiable equity goals, such as opening access to advanced courses. A school's ability to successfully operationalize that goal is dependent on the extent to which they embrace it as their own. They must review the data, engage their communities, and rethink their approach. They must learn how to do something different in order to achieve a new goal, and the principal must lead that learning. It is the job of principal supervisors to provide support, perhaps in accessing and analyzing data, finding examples of others who have done it, or helping to create a schoolwide professional learning plan. The strength of doing it this way ensures that not only will the school embrace the change as its own, but the inevitable opponents to an equity move will have a harder time pushing back on something that is championed by the educators within a school. And that means a transformation effort will be more likely to last.

A PORTFOLIO OF TOOLKITS

When Jen Cheatham was superintendent of Madison, Wisconsin, she instituted a school improvement planning that struck the right balance on the "loose–tight" continuum. She and her team were very clear with the board and community about what needed to be done. The diverse district of approximately 27,000 students in fifty schools needed a transformative equity agenda. Jen came to Madison after serving as a top leader in both San Diego, California, and Chicago, Illinois. When she arrived in 2013, the state had just taken away collective bargaining, social and racial justice organizations like the Urban League of Greater Madison were becoming increasingly vocal about the atrocious performance of Black students, and a big report about the entire county was published that laid bare the startling discrepancies in health and wellness indicators between Black and white residents. The time was right for a transformational equity minded leader who could organize a teaching and learning agenda. Jen had embarked on a comprehensive entry process when she first began, which gave her deep insight into the issues Madison faced. She also established multiple engagement processes with internal and external stakeholders, which built trust. The groundwork was laid for her to drive an equity agenda, which rested on adopting disciplined ways of working and learning. Decision-making processes were a crucial part of the plan.

After her entry process, Jen relied on educators within the system to develop a strategic planning framework that would improve practice and spark innovation. Her interest was not to get schools to simply follow the dictates of central office, but to strengthen adult practice and innovate in their own contexts within the framework established by the superintendent and board, with the deep input of stakeholders. Jen had also learned of the district's many strengths during her entry phase, but there was little coherence and too much pursuit of various initiatives. People were worn out by the chasing of bright shiny objects and needed a more authentic and comprehensive approach grounded in evidence-based practices and true collaboration. Due to the elimination of collective bargaining in the state of Wisconsin and the sidelining of educators under the previous administration, Jen knew that in order for her strategy to work, Madison educators had to lead the charge. The process also engendered trust between schools and her, as they could see Jen and her team listening to the people doing the tough work in schools and incorporating their views into the district's strategy.

Jen and the team determined three main goals for the system: raising academic achievement and narrowing gaps; changing school climate and culture; and ensuring access to a well-rounded educational experience. These goals were intended to be both holistic in speaking to the most important equity components of schools, and also able to counteract each other. Yes, increasing scores on standardized tests is important, but not at the expense of access to other educational experiences, and any real change happens in the midst of positive school climates and strong collaborative cultures. These three goals were then supposed to be realized by the district's theory of action, which rested on three pillars. The first was a more disciplined way of working with the school improvement plan (SIP) being the crux of a change effort. The second pillar was about functioning as one large learning community across the district. They needed to collectively learn together about things such as culturally and linguistically conscious instruction and racial equity. At her core, Jen Cheatham is an active learner, and she wanted the entire system to be deeply engaged in learning together. The third pillar focused on central office work. Schools were placed at the center and central office work was then designed to be in support of SIPs, not the other way around as is typical in too many districts. While central office signed off on SIPs, their job was to determine how to provide resources and break down barriers. Schools told the central office what their priorities should be rather than the other way around.

Once Jen had all of this in place, the actual transformation work had to happen in schools. This is where the portfolio of toolkits came in. She had a very deliberate approach to school improvement that began with having a strong leadership team, moved into collaborative teacher teams, and then tackled family engagement. The toolkits were designed to create a learning organization that rested on evidence-based practices that schools could implement within their own contexts. They helped schools strengthen decision-making processes so that their strategies to meet the three system goals would be more likely to succeed. Educators from across the system, with the help of outside experts, were involved in creating the toolkits, which increased their sense of ownership. Jen found a way to support schools on their learning and improvement journeys that fit their culture and context yet was within a tight framework with clear expectations and accountability. After six years of improved achievement, bold efforts to tackle equity and social justice, and an improved culture, Jen handed the reigns to the next leader who could take the system further.

The ingenuity of the decision-making system that Jen created was the deep attention to the learning process. Most leaders follow the rules of consistency and results. They don't embrace the complex work of creating learning environments, as that work can be quite messy. It's easier, to a certain point, to make decisions for people and then hold them accountable for results. Jen and her team were certainly focused on outcomes, while also being relentless in insisting that everyone in the district be constantly learning how to improve their practice, and she modeled that behavior regularly. Jen met with various constituent advisory groups on a regular basis to test out her thinking and triangulate the data she was gathering about the state of the system. This helped her learn about the real issues Madison was facing. She brought in outside help when needed and ensured that experts were in the right positions on her team to support the collective learning of others. The chiefs of schools and their teams meet for a half-day every Friday to calibrate their work around what they were learning from the field. Jen engaged her board in the learning process as well by having them meet one Saturday per quarter with her executive team and sometimes with various principals so they could hear about the real work in schools. Decision-making in Madison under Jen Cheatham wasn't about who had the authority to make decisions. Rather, it was about how a community can come together to make the right decisions for kids. In some districts, however, authority is the basis for contentiousness, and too often, negotiations with unions are the manifestations of that power struggle.

INTEREST-BASED NEGOTIATIONS

I have only worked in districts with employee associations. In the schoolhouse and throughout the system, they tend to have a lot of power. The contract dictates the length of the school day, the scheduling of adult time, and the workload of teachers. I am a firm believer in the role of unions in the American workplace, as employees need protections and due processes. I've also seen how unions can stifle innovation and thwart progress on equity goals. Too often, unions and district leaders, including the board, engage in contract negotiations with the traditional offer/counteroffer approach. The union asks for a percentage salary increase that's much higher than they know they'll get. The management team counteroffers with something much lower than they know they'll give. The two sides go back and forth and meet in the middle, with no one very happy, continued mistrust, and both sides simultaneously claiming victory and the ability to compromise. It's a standard approach that may work just fine during good economic times and can be a disaster when the coffers run dry. The dynamic created by this approach is another maintainer of the status quo, so leaders seeking to transform their systems need to learn to rewrite the rules of how they negotiate decisions.

Another approach that I've experienced, both as a system leader and as a superintendent, is interest-based bargaining. Interest-based negotiations change the dynamic between management and unions and allow for a different kind of conversation. Based on Fisher and Ury's work in the 1980s and 1990s in the Harvard Negotiations Project and described in "Getting to Yes,"[5] interest-based negotiation rewrites the rules of labor–management interactions. More importantly, it can fundamentally improve decision making processes for the entire system through a focus on shared principles, rather than positions. In Chapter 4, I'll discuss how an interest-based approach can lead to a better budget process.

Imagine if, rather than starting a negotiation with an employee association by offering a percentage increase, both sides spent time laying out why they want something, rather than just what they want. Both sides, for example, want teachers to feel valued by the system. Both sides want student achievement and learning to improve. Both sides want teachers to have opportunities to learn new skills. In a traditional negotiation, these elements of effective schools can play second fiddle to the contractual elements that are often discussed first. The percentage increase becomes the focus of the debate rather than the more important interest that both sides have of ensuring that teachers feel respected and valued by the system and will want to stay for their careers. There may be other ways of achieving those interests beyond just the percentage increase. Incentives can be created to reward additional responsibilities; teachers can be given increased opportunities to learn, lead, and collaborate. But if the dollar amount is the only thing discussed, labor and management may not get to those other approaches.

Interest-based processes require a lot of training and full commitment by all sides. Some superintendents are pressured by board members or other elected officials to squeeze as much as they can from unions. Employment contracts, much like the budget (more in Chapter 4) are symbols of the system's values and opportunities for political theater. Elected officials, including board members, who ran on holding teachers accountable or fiscal conservatism will seize the chance to criticize a leader who is seen to compromise too much. Union leaders, too, can be under the gun from their members to get as much as they possibly can, whatever the cost. These dynamics, which tend to garner more public attention than other issues, can put both sides in a difficult place. Yet when there's a true commitment to interest-based decision-making, any skepticism can be waylaid by the collaboration that ensues. Interest-based negotiations build trust, which is an essential ingredient of an equity agenda. The trust built up over time through being trained together and then coming to agreement on difficult issues provides a strong foundation upon which to build an equity agenda.

CONCLUSION

The one area of decision-making I have not yet addressed is community engagement. Chapter 7 provides strategies for working with families, students, and community members to move an equity agenda. And I make clear throughout this book that stakeholders must be a part of any effort to transform a system, and system leaders must have a comprehensive engagement strategy. The entry points for change management I describe in this book are not intended to be stand alone. Each works off the other in almost a fractal way—seemingly discrete parts of an organization that come together to create a beautiful whole.[6] The process of making decisions within a complex organization requires a leader to be thoughtful, deliberate, and transparent about how those parts fit together.

The main rule of decision-making to be rewritten is transparency and engagement. Public school systems are just that—public. They're not a private company; they'll be there much longer than any superintendent, and they serve the public, however messy that truth may be. Yes, the superintendent has authority and power, but that power should not be seen as a zero-sum game. In fact, when more people are involved in decision-making, the power to make real change grows exponentially. It's like a Marvel movie when the superhero realizes that they can't defeat the forces of evil alone, they need to rely on others' unique powers. A leader trying to transform a school system to be more equitable and socially just can sometimes feel like they're in such a movie. The ones that think they can do it alone, however, end up failing.

There are many decisions that have to be made when moving an equity agenda. From formal policies and contracts to process improvements that focus on adult learning in order to improve practice, leaders need a deliberate approach to collaboration and engagement. Expanding the power base by including more people is difficult, but it will lead to a better and longer-lasting solution. A superintendent who rewrites these rules will find that their stakes in the ground become deeper and more cemented when they involve others in decision-making. In fact, planting the flag in the ground of equity is just the first step. Inviting others to make the soil more fertile is what leads to transformation.

4

Resource Allocation According to Vision and Need

ONE YEAR WHEN I was superintendent in Montgomery County, Maryland, I presented a budget to the Board of Education with a $1.5 million increase for services to students who were or had been English language learners (ELLs). There were two pressing issues that drove this request: stagnant reading progress for ELLs in the elementary grades and a large influx of children from Central America, many of whom were unaccompanied minors. I wanted to address long-standing gaps in our approach to literacy and be prepared to meet the needs of a new, very vulnerable population. One of my board members, a retired former principal, asked where she could find the commensurate investment in Black children. This board member had been one of the first Black women principals in the district, was a leader in the local NAACP, and had been the head of the district's Alliance of Black School Educators. She was also very close with a group of veteran civil rights activists called the 1977 Coalition II, as they had first formed back then to demand changes to the system. As the district was still coming out of lean budget times and arguing with the county over funding levels, I offered few new budget items that year. My intent to shore up our approach to ELLs was based on a data-driven, proactive approach that would help us meet a growing need before it became a bigger challenge. I was trying to drive an equity agenda, which, at its core, means that those who need the most, get it.

In both private and public meetings, I shared with this board member and others the data behind my recommendation. I showed that our Black students' literacy achievement was steady, and that even though there was still a gap with white and Asian students, they outperformed our ELLs and Latinx students in general. I described how our new "focus" teachers were intended to support any and all students who needed help and would certainly be a part of the strategy for our Black students. But it wasn't enough. This board member wouldn't support an increased investment in ELLs unless an equal amount of money was in the budget for Black students. I realized after we had gone back and forth many times that we were having two different conversations. I was objectively looking at the data, our vision, and needs and doing what I considered to be the job of the superintendent by giving the board a fact-based spending plan. This board member was attending to her political interests by publicly showing that she was the champion for Black students in Montgomery County that she had always still been. That cause had gotten her elected to the board in the first place and had been a core part of her leadership and advocacy throughout her whole career. She wasn't about to just follow the relatively new, white superintendent of schools when there was a clear political gain for her.

Some of the most challenging, time-consuming, and consequential decisions a leader makes concern resource allocation. They directly affect everyone in the system, and new investments can be risky if educators need to learn new practices. Budgets are an opportunity for political theater, as board members and the local funding authority have distinct causes they may have campaigned on or constituents with certain interests. Employee associations have their demands and desires. Parents typically only understand and support what they see happen at their child's school and don't always trust the opaqueness of the system's decision-making processes. And it all takes place in the public eye, as the media and public tend to pay more attention to budgets than many other things.

I don't know if I could've done something different to get this board member to support my $1.5 million request, other than simply allocate the same amount to her cause. Moreover, there may have been some political gain for me in showing that I was an independent leader who would follow the data, needs, and vision and not get caught up in political concerns. Regardless, within a $2.4 billion operating budget a $1.5 million investment was a drop in the bucket that increased attention to the students' needs and represented only part of a comprehensive strategy to meet them.

Frankly, I can't even remember whether the money stayed in the budget, given how miniscule the amount was, but I do know that this board member's support for me dropped, which had consequences later.

I offer the example as it shows the typical way superintendents and boards engage in budget deliberations. The standard approach is for superintendents to spend a few months in the fall working with their schools and central office administrators to develop a budget. They may meet with board leadership and perhaps the fiscal committee during this time. Then they might present an overview to employee associations and other community groups to get their input and support. Early in the new year the superintendent presents their budget to the fiscal committee, whose meetings are public and often attended by non-committee members, who then reviews, adjusts, and sends it to the full board. The superintendent and their team then present the budget in public, supported by numerous PowerPoint slides rife with inspiration and data. For about a month the board and superintendent engage in some back and forth until they settle on a spending plan for the next year. By the springtime, the budget goes either to the public for a referendum or the local funding authority for their review and approval. State budget allocations typically don't come through until the late spring, so final numbers may be unknown. Throughout this whole time, various constituents and interest groups are lobbying board members and other elected officials. By June, the final budget is passed, school ends and summer planning begins. As my wife said to me after my first year as superintendent in Stamford, "You spend four months building the budget and four months cutting the budget; when do you do anything else?"

This chapter is about how to rewrite the rules of resource allocation. The budget is the most public symbol of the system's priorities and values. Yet money is not the only resource that a leader has to drive an equity-based transformation agenda. It's one of three, the other two being time and talent. Since people make up at least 80 percent of a school system's budget, how they're organized to meet the collective vision and system's needs is the key role of superintendents. In this chapter, I'll describe various processes that superintendents can use to drive an equity agenda through the strategic use of time, the deployment of talent, and the allocation of funds. By using interest-based approaches to decision-making, collaboration, and data, leaders can chart a bold course to transform their system. In addition to my own experiences as a superintendent developing budgets, reorganizing time, and focusing on people, I'll describe how two superintendents strategically reallocated resources to address long-standing equity issues. Rudy Crew's chancellor's district in New York City in the mid-1990s was a bold and successful effort to increase investments and consolidate authority in the lowest performing schools in order to increase student achievement. Damien Pattenaude in Renton, Washington, has taken a similar approach twenty-five years later that is leading to improved outcomes for that district's most vulnerable students. Strategic resource allocation is the main lever to pull for superintendents who seek to transform their systems through an equity lens. The challenge is to rewrite the rules around how time is organized, talent is deployed, and funds are invested.

SCHEDULES ARE THE BLACK BOX OF SCHOOL REFORM

Ask educators what they feel they need more of, and they often answer "time." At the end of professional development sessions when they go around the room and give "plusses" and "deltas," time will invariably be one of the deltas. Too often the bell rings at the end of class when a teacher is in mid-sentence. The allocation of approximately seven hours of time over one hundred and eighty school days a year is one of the most consequential aspects of school leadership. That process reflects their values and those of the system and is subject to all of the complexity of decision-making as described in Chapter 3. Contracts with employee associations can dictate the length of a class period and how much time teachers spend with students, collaborate with peers, plan lessons, and are assigned to other school duties. Federal and state regulations determine how much additional support certain students are supposed to get during the school day. Ultimately, how time is allocated will determine whether a desired change in adult practice that improves teaching and learning will actually last.

The equity imperative regarding allocating time within a school rests on two variables: the need for adults to improve their practice to better meet the needs of students and the need to support the most vulnerable students without relegating them to low-level courses. Leaders must consider both of these factors when scheduling. Improving adult practice requires that adults be constantly learning with colleagues, so leaders must schedule time for collaboration. Helping students requires providing them with the right kind of support during an already busy day.

Organizing for Adult Learning

The true test of a leader is how they organize adults to learn from each other how to improve their practice. While Chapter 5 is all about talent management and will delve deeper into this topic, adult learning is also a resource allocation issue as it entails finding time and distributing people and may have financial implications as well. Too often, adult learning in districts and schools is dictated from the central office and linked to a new initiative or a program requirement. Sometimes these sessions are "turnkey," or "train the trainer," whereby a cadre of school personnel are taught how to distribute the information to colleagues in their schools. Or, they're one session "sit-and-gits," where a central office administrator or outside expert spends an hour or so telling teachers about the new initiative or product. These standard approaches are why teachers tend to say that they don't like professional development that comes from the district. Rewriting the rule of adult learning is one of the most important tasks of a system leader and largely concerns the allocation of time and talent.

Within every school building there are educators eager to develop new skills and apply new knowledge. There are also various levels of expertise, both in content and facilitation. Too often these resources are squandered when principals aren't encouraged and taught to develop professional learning communities (PLCs). Collaborative and structured adult learning has been shown to improve adult practice and student learning.[1] Yet, American teachers tend to spend more time instructing students and less time learning with and from colleagues than almost any other teachers throughout the world.[2] Chapter 5 will describe how PLCs and adult learning need to be organized to lead to improved practice, but here I consider how a superintendent can rewrite the rules to ensure that in every school, time is allocated so that adults are learning with and from each other.

When I was superintendent in Stamford, we implemented PLCs in every one of our twenty schools. Some schools were already organized for adults to learn collaboratively, and we just had to support their ongoing efforts. Others were eager or willing to do so, and we had to coach and guide so that they succeeded. A few were more resistant and skeptical of just about anything that the new superintendent said, so we had to create some accountability mechanisms. Regardless of the readiness and desire of the school, I had to put structures in place centrally to ensure that within each school, adults were organized to learn from and with each other. Teachers had already expressed dissatisfaction with the standard approach to professional development, and they wanted more time to collaborate with peers. Hence, I had an opportunity to respond to their feedback by instituting an evidence-based, effective strategy. Here was a rare opportunity for a win–win.

In order to ensure that PLCs were being implemented in alignment with evidence-based practices, we took a deliberately "loose–tight" approach. We spent a lot of time developing resources and helping school leaders, including teachers, with their PLC implementation strategy.[3] Our PLC cycle was tight, as each one was expected to analyze data, look at student work, examine instruction, assess student progress, and reflect. And we provided training to teacher leaders to learn how to facilitate the PLC cycle. But we didn't dictate the content, as long as it was linked to an instructional improvement goal. Our investment was in the systems intended to support adult learning at the school level. Through a district steering committee that included teachers, training, monitoring, and differentiated supports, we invested time in the creation of structures that would engender improved adult practice. Rather than try to control the time that adults spent learning new skills and knowledge, we were focused on creating the space for them to do so. It's a subtle but powerful shift. Superintendents should not try to control what every adult is learning in every school. They can, however, insist that there's an ecosystem for learning within every school that is based on the school's needs and vision. When time is spent doing that, it's much more likely to be effective and lead to improved student learning.

Organizing for Increased Student Supports

During my first year as superintendent in Montgomery County, Maryland, I asked every member of the Executive Leadership Team to shadow a student at one of our twenty-five high schools. I spent the day with a junior named David. While I had always invested considerable time visiting schools and talking with students and teachers, I hadn't been in a high school for a full day since I graduated Mamaroneck High School in 1987. It was eye-opening and exhausting. What struck me most was how time was used. From the first bell at 7:45 a.m., David and I attended classes in forty-seven-minute increments with a few minutes in between. Some of the courses were boring, others engaging, and a few teachers were clearly trying to impress me. What I couldn't get my head around was how David, for one hundred and eighty days of the year, had to switch his mental model every forty-seven minutes, seven times per day. For every class he had to be mentally prepared. Does he like the teacher? How are his peers? Is he confident about his grasp of the material? Did he complete his homework? Does he know the answers when called upon? Is he ready for the test? Rinse and repeat. By mid-day I was wiped out, and by the end of the day I had remembered very little content but left with much more insight into why high school students tend to be much less engaged in school than elementary students.[4] When we organize school around the movement of students within discrete chunks of time spent focused on transmitting facts and figures about one subject, teenagers have to do all they can just to keep up with the teacher. How time is used in all schools will determine whether students are engaged, accelerated, supported, or bored to tears.

Schedules are the black box of school improvement. What services and supports go to which kids and when is the essence of equity. Once adult learning time is established, the precious resource of student contact time becomes a key determinant in students' success. Schools that receive additional resources (people and money) for serving students who may have a 504 or an IEP, be ELLs, or be eligible for free and reduced price meals have an additional challenge of organizing adults to deliver all of those services and supports. Such a school might also have a reading or math specialist to coach teachers and provide additional support to students. Moreover, Title 1, ELL, and Individuals With Disabilities Act (IDEA) dollars often go toward buying more programs and materials, all of which need to fit into an already jam-packed day and can exacerbate the narrowing of curriculum by limiting music, the arts, physical education, and even recess. How time is used is the true measure of school leadership, and superintendents would do well to attend to the details of this precious resource, as it portends a school's potential for success.

There are a few basic elements of how time should be used within a school to drive increased student achievement. Superintendents should insist that principal supervisors adhere to evidence-based practices through model schedules and peer coaching. Teachers also need to be coached and taught about how to best allocate the time they have with students. Is it all whole-group instruction, or do students have opportunities for small-group, partner, or individual work? How much time is spent on direct instruction at the beginning of a lesson, and how much is on practicing and applying new skills or knowledge? Are certain subjects taught at the beginning of the day rather than the end? How much time is spent on material distribution, going to the bathroom, and discipline? Are teachers being interrupted regularly by announcements from the main office? There is, in fact, no one magic way of allocating time within a school day. What's necessary is a deliberate review and collective understanding of how it is being used to maximize student learning and achievement. A collective review of the use of time within a school is also a great opportunity for shared decision-making.[5]

When driving an equity agenda, superintendents must insist that school leaders engage their staff in reviewing and designing their use of time with the goal of increasing student learning and maximizing core instruction. Too often, students get pulled out of class for interventions, when that can not only disrupt the flow of the day for the child but cause them to lose precious time when the teacher is delivering important content. Also, it can stigmatize the child by highlighting their "otherness" to peers. Good first instruction is more important than anything when improving student achievement and learning,[6] so the reliance on out-of-class interventions may not achieve the desired result. The nature of too many school and system leaders is to layer on more staff and programs in an attempt to meet the needs of students. It's easier to just ask for more rather than to consider whether what you're doing in the first place is having the desired effect. There may be a need to include intervention time into a daily schedule,[7] as some students will need additional support. But again, how that time is used is the key. Have the specialist and the grade level or subject teacher met to analyze results of an assessment that led to the determination that intervention was needed? Have they agreed on an explicit instructional strategy that they'll both reinforce? When will they review results of the intervention and readjust? How will they leverage the expertise of central office personnel? Without considering how those precious resources are used within a tight framework of what excellent instruction looks like, leaders run the risk of perpetuating the status quo.

PEOPLE MAKE THE ALL THE DIFFERENCE

Since more than 80 percent of a school system's budget funds people, the process of distributing and assigning talent to task is an extremely important resource allocation function for a superintendent. Chapter 5 will discuss talent management in depth and will build on themes and ideas raised here, but people should be seen as the greatest resource a leader has and part of the allocation methodology. In this section, I'll touch on how to distribute and assign people within a system, and in Chapter 5 I'll discuss how to manage them once allocated.

The standard approach to allocating people within schools is based on state rules, district policies, contracts with employee associations, and tradition. At the school level, principals assign teachers to classes based on their knowledge of their skills, seniority, the schedule, and even politics. Other employees in schools, such as paraprofessionals, specialists, mental health professionals, secretaries, librarians, custodians, and cafeteria staff are often assigned to the school from central office and may be the only person in their role. Even a principal's administrative team may not be of their choosing. When I was in Stamford, I did not allow principals to hire their own assistant principals. I wanted assistant principals to become principals and be mentored and taught by leaders with a different skill set than theirs. And some principals needed help in certain areas. While not every principal liked my decision initially, most of them came to understand the value of the strategy, and many of the assistant principals went on to become great principals.

Given that a principal can't always determine who their people are, central office can play a role in how talent is allocated throughout the system and within schools, especially when driving an equity agenda. As Chapter 5 will go deeper into talent management, the main point to consider is how the rules of distribution are determined. When trying to transform a school system through an equity lens, leaders must focus on the few things that directly relate to improving student learning and achievement. Great teaching is one of those few factors. Thus, how personnel are allocated relative to the system's vision and needs is an essential component of a leader's transformation agenda. Central office leaders can play a role in ensuring that those who need the most effective educators get them.

Two of the levers that central office can pull to allocate staff according to vision and need are contracts with employee groups and the supervision of principals. Contracts must create the conditions for employees to be assigned to and within schools based on performance and a school's needs. This means that teacher evaluation processes should take into account all of the domains of a teacher's effectiveness. This includes, of course, student performance indicators, and should also consider an educator's attention to issues such as SEL and equity, as well as their leadership, personal growth, and collaboration with others. If teachers have been properly evaluated, that data should then be used to assign them to the schools and students who need them most. Unfortunately, the rules around teacher evaluation processes and procedures need to be rewritten to support professional growth and learning, as I'll discuss in Chapter 5.

Principal supervision is, yet again, an important factor in ensuring that talent is allocated according to vision and need. Whenever I work with system leaders on their transformation strategy, I always ask them their definition of equity. Some can recite the high-level language in policy or the strategic plan, others state that it's meeting the needs of all students. I then ask them who assigns teachers to students. Typically, they stare at me blankly and maybe exchange side glances with their colleagues. One may pipe up and say, "principals." I then ask how they know that the most effective teachers are assigned to the most vulnerable students. More blank stares. I then tell them that all of their aspirational language about equity doesn't mean a thing if they're not making the most important equity move they can make in their systems, which is to assign the best teachers to the students who need them most.

The superintendent, central office leaders, and principal supervisors should not be actually assigning teachers to students. Principal supervisors should, however, work with their principals to ensure that the best teachers are working with the most vulnerable students. No increase in staffing, reduction in class size, purchase of new materials, implementation of new curriculum or professional development is a better use of resources than the distribution of talent. Any leader seeking to transform their system through an equity lens needs to start by asking whether the right people are in the right places before they ask for increased investments in programs and products.

MONEY MAKES THE WORLD GO ROUND

Superintendents have a sacred trust with citizens when it comes to spending money. In most districts, local tax dollars comprise the bulk of the budget. Districts, of course, receive state and federal funds according to their enrollment of students who receive free and reduced price meals or qualify for additional services. But most residents don't pay much attention to the details of the funding source as they argue for certain investments or cry foul over perceived wasteful spending. Many elected officials are no different, especially if they have the power to fund the school budget. Superintendents run a greater risk of getting fired over a financial impropriety than they do over chronically low test scores, so they have to be extra cognizant of the budget. When I first got to Stamford, I was told that my predecessor wasn't very interested in the budget and left his assistant superintendent for business to appear at some of the hearings in front of the city boards of finance and representatives, who approved the spending plan. I didn't have much of a financial background, but school system budgets aren't very complicated. So, I spent a weekend going through every line of the budget book and wrote questions in the margins if I didn't understand what the money was being used for. My team then provided explanations, which we used to update the book before we went in front of the boards, under the assumption that my commonsense questions were likely to be asked by them too. As I stood in front of the boards, I was able to answer every question and curveball they threw at me. I was showing them that I took seriously my role as fiscal steward, and I was showing the staff, the media, and observers that I wouldn't leave it to someone else to stand up for the funds that I believed our children and schools needed. More importantly, I was able to use the budget hearing process to tell a story about equity, the needs of our students, and my vision for the system.

The budget is a manifestation of a system's values. By presenting it to community leaders, stakeholders, staff, and families, a superintendent has the opportunity to convey their beliefs about what students need and their vision for the system. When giving it to the board of education and then the elected funding authority, a leader shows their intention to organize and fight for their schools. When driving an equity-based transformation agenda, the stakes are raised, as people are likely to support one side or the other. Proponents of equity will argue for their particular interests while opponents will obfuscate theirs by asking a lot of questions and requesting more information. Superintendents have to then rewrite the rules of budgeting by paying close attention to the budget development process and the engagement of stakeholders.

AN INTEREST-BASED APPROACH

In Chapter 3, I described how interest-based bargaining can help superintendents make decisions with employee associations. Those same principles can be used to develop an annual budget. Typically, a superintendent formally submits their budget to the board in the late winter. They've likely had discussions with individual board members, leadership, and perhaps the budget committee on the range of the proposed increase and the inclusion of particular items. After submitting the budget and presenting it to the board, there will be time for public comment and then a lot of back and forth among board members, some of whom will want to address pet issues or respond to constituents. This dynamic can't be fully avoided, but it can be controlled to maintain appropriate "above the line" and "below the line" behavior.

I chose to take a different tack. I would meet with my board during the summer, prior to the internal budget development processes that began during the fall. This meeting was intended to determine the board's interests for the upcoming year so that the budget I presented six months later reflected their values, not their positions. The rule of horse trading and micromanaging was rewritten to engender collaboration and maintain appropriate roles. Board members would spend a good amount of time sharing their interests—*why* they wanted something rather than *what* they wanted. Class size is a perfect example of an issue that is perennially debated during typical budget negotiations. Parents and teachers advocate for small class sizes, thinking that it will mean more attention given to their child and be more manageable. Board members are responsive and tell the superintendent to lower them a certain amount. The superintendent and their team know that there is limited research showing that smaller classes have a big impact on student achievement. Yet the conventional wisdom and politics hold sway, and the superintendent has to lower class size in some grades or for some students. Meanwhile, other necessary investments are put off for another year.

Missing from this debate over class size is any discussion of how students' individual needs will be met within a class with a few less students than the previous year. Will teachers be trained in formative assessments or have access to better data so that they can measure student progress more facilely and intervene quicker? Will new materials or technology be purchased so that teachers can differentiate instruction? Will teachers know better how to meet the needs of ELLs or SWDs with fewer students in their class? It's not likely that these issues will be discussed, as the promise of a smaller class is enough for many people to not look under the hood.

For a superintendent who knows that smaller class sizes only get you so much, an interest-based approach to budget development can meet the board's need to respond to constituents while also allowing the leader to lead. During the late summer meeting to determine the board's interests regarding the next year's budget, it would be perfectly reasonable to list "increase individualized attention and differentiation" as something that the superintendent should address. There are more ways of achieving this than simply lowering class size, and by framing the issue in terms of why the board wants to see something in the budget, the superintendent has the opportunity to figure out how to achieve this.

When using an interest-based approach to develop a budget, it's essential to publicly affirm the board's interests on a regular basis. Stakeholders have the right to know what to expect and how leadership is investing tax dollars. System leaders also have the responsibility to regularly check their assumptions and proposals against the board's publicly stated interests throughout the development process. Then, when the budget is publicly presented to the board, the superintendent must show how their proposal is aligned to those interests, and individual board members cannot include new items. Working this way, both entities are able to fulfill their appropriate leadership roles and collaborate on what can too often be a contentious process.

A board's interests should also shape internal budget development and collaboration procedures. Every year, central office program administrators and school principals submit their wish lists to the budget office for hopeful inclusion in the recommendation to the superintendent, who then will make decisions and send it along to the board of education. Administrators have to justify the proposed expenditure and then show how it will meet a particular outcome. The budget office sifts and winnows this list until something reasonable can be sent on to the superintendent. Compromises are made, and no one gets everything they want, but everyone mostly understands why their request can't be met this year. Sometimes, a principal will rally their community to advocate for something when the budget eventually goes to the board. Depending on the political power of that school, the board may listen, which could compromise the superintendent's ability to fund an equity agenda. A typical budget development process runs this risk. An interest-based and collaborative approach can mitigate it.

When a board's interests are established early in the process, program and school administrators can then align their requests to them. Once they've done so, a collaborative decision-making process can be a filter that determines what makes it into the next year's spending plan. When I became superintendent of Montgomery County, Maryland, I was struck by the deep collaborative deliberations over the budget among the three employee associations (teachers, support professionals, and administrators), the central office staff, and parent representatives. There was an ethos about working together to determine the priorities and needs for the next year. While this could be tedious and lengthy, it was essential when difficult decisions needed to be made. The collaboration also ensured a united front when the budget went to the Board of Education and the County Council. Each group was responsible for informing their constituents about the budget request, and representatives would testify in front of the elected officials to show their support. Not everything I or another group wanted made it into the budget. But there wasn't a likelihood of radical changes. Moreover, the unified front was a compelling message to the entire community that their tax dollars would be spent well in support of students.

KNOW WHEN TO NOT BE NICE

While collaboration and an interest-based approach are preferable, they're not always practical. Sometimes the conditions demand that a leader step in and do what's needed to serve children. One of my favorite guilty pleasure movies is *Roadhouse*. In it, Patrick Swayze plays a bouncer at a bar who's legendary for being able to take down anyone, despite his diminutive size. As he trains his fellow bouncers, he tells them to always be nice, until, of course, it's time to not be nice. Much like Sun Tzu said, it's always better to not engage in a battle, but if you're going to, choose one you're likely to win.[8] When it comes to the budget, a superintendent is more likely to engender support by building coalitions and attending to local context. Sometimes, however, the situation demands swift and bold action. Sometimes, a superintendent can't afford to be nice.

When Rudy Crew was chancellor of New York City in the mid to late 1990s he may not have watched Patrick Swayze or read Sun Tzu, but he channeled their energies by establishing the Chancellor's District. Rudy Crew rewrote the rules in NYC of how to allocate resources to better serve students. Rudy became chancellor in 1995 under Mayor Rudy Giuliani, a notorious streetfighter. The previous chancellor, Ramon Cortines, was a great teaching and learning leader and a true gentleman, but NYC needed someone a little more brash and bold to lead the system during the advent of the standards era. Rudy Crew fit the bill perfectly.

At the time, NYC was divided into thirty-two districts, each with their own Board of Education and superintendents. Decentralized control and authority was baked into the system. However, there was a clear equity issue that was becoming more apparent. Increased attention to student achievement data and academic standards laid bare the stark disparities among different groups of students. For generations, students of color and poor students languished in underperforming schools, and no chancellor had been able to penetrate the local control that perpetuated these inequities. Rudy was dead set on doing something about it. He used the previously untapped authority of the chancellor's office to eventually take over fifty-eight low-performing elementary schools. He removed them from their geographic district and established a Chancellor's District dedicated to lifting the performance of the lowest achieving schools in the system.

Rudy's strategy was fairly straightforward: use the authority you have to allocate resources so that those who need more services and supports get them. It also bucked the nascent reform movement's outcry over deadweight bureaucracy and centralized control.[9] While school systems are loosely coupled entities, as discussed in previous chapters, sometimes a leader has to step in and tighten the rope between the central office and schools. Rudy asserted that he and his team could do it better by placing the schools under his control and giving them what he thought they needed. Investments were made in core curriculum, professional development, extra staffing, smaller class sizes and extended day programs. Each school followed a prescribed schedule and "Model of Excellence." The additional resources had an impact: Fourth-grade reading scores increased, and gaps were narrowed, although these schools still lagged behind others in the city.[10] We don't know what would've happened if Rudy had stayed chancellor, as Giuliani pushed him out over a disagreement about vouchers. But he showed that a top system leader can increase student achievement by taking bold action to invest in evidence-based school improvement strategies.

A PRODIGAL SON RETURNS

Damien Pattenaude, superintendent of Renton, Washington, leads a district a fraction of the size of NYC, with about sixteen thousand students in twenty-three schools. Twenty years after Rudy Crew established the Chancellor's District by strategically investing in schools, Damien has made similar leadership moves. As a former standout basketball player and graduate of Renton High School with deep ties to the community, he has gone about it in a very different way, but with a similar laser-like focus on insisting that resources support evidence-based strategies intended to improve learning and achievement for the system's most vulnerable students.

When Damien started in Renton in 2001, he thought he would teach and coach basketball. But mentors saw something in him, and he quickly started his leadership journey. Damien became the principal of the high school he graduated from, then an assistant superintendent, and by 2016 was named the superintendent-elect. When he ascended to the top job the next year, Damien was ready to take on the equity challenges facing Renton and begin the transformation process.

Renton, just outside of Seattle; is about a quarter each white, Asian/Pacific Islander, and Hispanic; 16 percent Black; and the rest Native American and multiracial. While the free and reduced price meals rate is 47 percent, the area is gentrifying as housing prices increase. The schools and communities aren't mixed, with one area, Skyway, being the poorest in all of King County. When Damien was a chief of schools, one of his elementary schools, Lakeridge, received a federal School Improvement Grant, designating it a "SIG" school. During the Obama/Duncan administration such schools were determined to be in need of improvement and were given additional resources. Jessica Granger, the principal, quickly instituted a series of reforms based on everything we know works to improve schools. It was a textbook approach grounded in her own instructional leadership: teacher learning and collaboration, intentional scheduling of the day, rich curriculum, regular assessments, and a culture committed to equity and excellence. The results were substantial, so when Damien became superintendent-elect, he convinced his boss to spread the model, and when he took on the top job, he tapped Jessica to make it work.

The first three schools that became part of the West Hill initiative were given specific additional resources related to time, talent, and funds. But the main resource that has helped these schools improve is the dedicated, focused attention of Jessica as chief of schools. They were given full-time counselors; professional learning communities were established in every school; and literacy and math labs with coaches were implemented. In addition, Damien negotiated with the teacher's association to waive certain aspects of the contract if the staff voted to do so, and to allow priority transfers out and no involuntary placements. Damien didn't pursue improvement simply by giving more resources. He created an ecosystem of supports to ensure that the schools could actually carry out their transformation strategies.

Damien was able to sell the West Hill Now model to the community by making the data public and leveraging his relationships and reputation. Everyone knew Skyway was the neediest area of the county. But no one had shown heat maps of the extent of the poverty, lack of access to health care, and inadequacy of social services. Given that Renton's diversity isn't reflected in its housing patterns or schools, it was clear that something needed to be done to support the students and families in this area. Moreover, according to Damien, as a Black superintendent who was raised in Renton, he was the perfect messenger to garner support among the community, the board, and the principals. Equity-based resource allocation is about prioritization and politics. Damien had clear priorities and the political acumen to make it work.

In addition to the internal reworking of schedules, curriculum, professional learning, and roles and responsibilities, Damien has brought in outside help. The Gates Foundation has taken notice of what's happening in Renton and is studying it. The Ballmer Foundation has established a nonprofit to help coordinate and provide wrap-around services for students and families. Each of the schools has a designated outside expert who helps them with their transformation efforts around mathematics and social-emotional learning. Yet the work has been harder than he anticipated. Damien knew it would take time and understood the primacy of the principal's role. But in one of the schools the principalship has turned over more than he would like, and the other principals require a lot of support and coaching from Jessica. Thus, the resources dedicated to the schools aren't just found in the school's staffing, budget, and schedule. They're also in the time that Damien, Jessica, and others spend to ensure the success of the initiative. Transformation doesn't just happen. It's like a fire that needs to be tended to and constantly stoked; otherwise, the flame may go out.

The West Hill Now model in Renton is similar to Rudy Crew's Chancellor's District in that it reflects the bold action of a superintendent who feels the urgency to act in order to rectify inequities. Both leaders reallocated resources to improve adult practice and student learning. Damien's approach differed, however, in that it rested in specific principles rather than a distinct program. Where Rudy had his "model of excellence" for everyone to follow with fidelity, Damien and Jessica have embraced the notion that there are some nonnegotiable principles that schools have to organize themselves around. And at the center of it all is a great school leader. As student achievement has increased in the West Hill Now schools, the practices have spread to other schools in the system. PLCs are now everywhere, as school staffs have agreed to contract waivers. So too is the focus of Damien and his team on principal supervision. Through this process of reallocating resources to ensure that those who need the most get it, Damien and his team have developed a comprehensive strategy around managing the system's performance. His theory of action that drives an equity-based transformation agenda is not to dictate what everybody does. Rather, Damien is abundantly clear about the nonnegotiable stakes in the ground that he expects to see in every school, he has allocated the resources for schools to invest as they organize around those stakes, and he's created the system to regularly monitor and support schools. Damien and his team have achieved the right balance on the "loose–tight" continuum.

CONCLUSION

One thing I've learned as a nonprofit CEO these past six years is that managing a small, approximately $4 million budget can be more complex than the $2.4 billion one I had in MCPS. I have much more flexibility with my current budget without the strictures of federal and state regulations, union contracts, and local politics. Decisions and adjustments can be made quickly and other than following generally accepted accounting practice rules and having a clean annual audit, I have only my board to answer to. But I must constantly measure whether our investments are getting the necessary return. We have to calculate expected margins and understand where the market is going. Philanthropy provides no guarantees and can be fickle, and even when I do raise some money, I need a sustainability plan as it will go away in a year or two.

Every time I choose to spend money on something that I think will pay off I'm taking a risk because I won't get those funds back the next year.

In school districts there are guarantees, even when difficult cuts need to be made. The district isn't going anywhere. In a nonprofit or a business, there are no guarantees. I have to constantly manage cash flow with an eye toward stability and innovation. How much do I need in reserves if there's a downturn (like the pandemic)? How much can I invest in a new idea before we expect to see a return? What's the minimal viable product that I can put out to test whether our ideas are good? How long will my staff stay if there aren't the kind of growth opportunities that exist in large organizations?

It's a very different kind of complexity than a school district budget, and I love it. It allows for creativity and innovation. I can run with a great idea and see it thrive or fail based on my own hard work and ability to motivate my team. There's very little that I have to negotiate or that stands in my way. It can be stressful, sure, but rewarding as well. School districts operate in a very different paradigm. The rules are set and followed accordingly every year. The opportunities for innovation and creativity may be scarce, but they can be found.

The allocation of people within a school and a district allows for more flexibility than some leaders may think. Toward the end of my time in Stamford we negotiated a clause in the contract that staff schedules could be staggered. My idea was that not every adult needed to be in the building at the same time from 8:00 in the morning until 3:00 in the afternoon. Why not have social workers come in and leave two hours later than teachers, which would be more family friendly? Reading and math specialists could do the same and provide support for students or offer professional development for teachers. Some may choose to work a staggered schedule because it fit better with their commute or childcare responsibilities. It would also lower costs, as we wouldn't have to pay stipends for working extra hours. A staggered schedule could also provide leadership opportunities for teachers or assistant principals. Unfortunately, none of the principals enacted this clause, as I wanted to do a pilot and slow roll out, and then I left the system. But the idea was an example of how to creatively use the tools you have to reallocate resources toward a desired end.

Title dollars are another example of how there can be more opportunities for innovation than some may think. State departments are notorious for restricting how these monies are spent. They put the federal guidelines through their own filters and present to districts limited options to choose from. When the district director responsible for applying for title funds goes to the state website, they'll find a drop-down menu based on the state's interpretation rather than the actual law. One classic example of this is the purchase of washing machines for schools. We've seen too many stories of the principal who's hailed for raising outside funds so that their vulnerable students and families can have clean clothes. And they should be, as school leaders who go above and beyond deserve recognition. But what's left out of the story is that they could have used Title 1 dollars to purchase laundry equipment in the first place, if only the state and district had told them it was allowable.

System leaders, especially superintendents of schools, have an obligation to create the conditions for success. When it comes to allocating resources, leaders certainly have to follow the rules so they don't get in trouble. But they must also find opportunities for schools to innovate and be creative. By being absolutely clear on the nonnegotiable stakes in the ground, supporting principals and holding them accountable, and stepping in where necessary, leaders can drive an equity-based transformation agenda.

5

Talent Management: How to Find, Engage, and Keep Great Educators

WHEN I WAS first hired as a teacher in Brooklyn, New York, the assistant principal, Judy, looked at me quizzically and asked, "What do you know?" Due to having enough undergraduate credits in both English and history, I qualified for a provisional license that allowed me to teach either subject to high school students with special needs, as it was a shortage area. The school was about to enroll adolescents labeled severely emotionally disturbed, and I had recent experience with that population from working in a group home when I lived in California. Plus, I stood nearly six feet, five inches, and the school needed somebody who could handle students who acted out a lot. When Judy took over the school when the principal who hired me retired, her initial question became somewhat of a running joke between us, as it was clear that, in fact, I knew very little about teaching.

Judy knew it would be bad for students and for me to give me a full class as soon as I started. The school was scheduled on a quarter system, so for the first ten weeks of the year I was placed with expert teachers who I could both help and learn from. I was also given lunch and hall duties, which enabled me to get to know a lot of the students in our small high school. I was assigned to a professional learning community, something the faculty had established by voting to waive a clause in the contract. By the time I was given my own class in the second quarter, I still didn't know much, but I had a picture of what good teaching and classroom management looked like, I had relationships with many of my students, and I knew most of the faculty.

As my time in the school went on, Judy and I developed a good relationship, and she helped me become a solid teacher and a teacher leader. Yet, during my time at the school, I was struck by something that has stayed with me throughout my career. Every teacher was considered the same, according to entrenched rules and contracts. Despite the clear differences among teachers' knowledge, skills, effort, and impact, they were one part of a machine. Judy's differentiated approach toward me was in spite of the rules of the system, not because of them. It was also an early lesson in how great principals bend the system's rules to their school's needs.

Weisberg and colleagues describe in *The Widget Effect*[1] how treating everyone the same in schools and systems has led to ineffective teachers staying in classrooms while excellence is rarely acknowledged or rewarded. While I take issue with some of their positions about the utility of tying standardized test scores to measures of teacher effectiveness, the core of their argument is hard to deny. Certainly, schools are complex entities that require disparate parts to work in concert toward a collective goal. Teachers can't simply do their own thing, at least when it comes to how a school is organized (although they can do whatever they want within the confines of their classrooms, which is, in fact, a large problem and a story for another day). For a school to work there must be rules, guidelines and standard operating procedures. Yet, as a young teacher, I could see that rigid adherence to those rules also stifled creativity. In fact, the realization that the system breeds mediocrity inspired me to go to graduate school, driven by the question of how to change the very systems that adults operate within so that students could be served better.

This chapter is about talent management. The rule that needs to be rewritten is one of moving beyond widgets. Great leaders find, develop, nurture, support, and hold accountable others. There is no way to run an effective school or system without activating talent toward a collective vision. Jim Collins's mantra of having "the right people on the bus,"[2] may be repeated in opening day staff meetings across the country. But it's an empty promise, as schools aren't designed to quickly move people on or off. As discussed in Chapter 4, since more than 80 percent of most school systems' budgets is comprised of people, managing and leading them well is the only way to achieve shared goals. They are the largest resource at a leader's disposal, and transformation happens through their actions.

Every one of the tenets described in previous chapters rests on the effective management of talent. To deliver rich content in an engaging way to diverse groups of students, people need to rise to the challenge and improve their practice. Values drive one's commitment to an organization and must be activated within a shared vision for what children should know and be able to do, and for what adults must do to support that. Collective leadership and decision-making requires that people within the system agree to work together toward that shared vision and learn how to do so. And effective and efficient resource allocation rests on the ability to assign talent to task. Talent management, in fact, is the glue that holds a system together.

In this chapter, I describe how system leaders should rewrite the rules of talent management. Processes to recruit, hire, develop, and support staff so that they achieve collective goals are described. The supervision of principals and alignment of central office work to enable effective talent management are also addressed. Examples from Highline, Washington, and the work of the Urban Schools Human Capital Academy will shed some light on these ideas. There is no one way to manage talent, as contexts, cultures, and written agreements differ among districts. Leaders can, however, be more likely to transform their system by applying a few key principles to how people are led.

FIRST DO NO HARM

When I'm asked about the school experience of my own children, I often half-joke that they're "just-add-water kids," in "first-do-no-harm-schools." My two sons and daughter have grown up in a stable, loving home with all the trappings of being part of upper-middle-class suburban society. Yes, there are many such students who struggle in school, and I don't want to diminish the individual needs of any child. But my children simply don't need a great school and top-tier teachers as much as other young people do. Sure, it would be wonderful if they were in engaging classes every minute, wrapped up in lessons and activities that stimulated their minds while they developed new skills. Some of their teachers have been wonderful, caring, and highly skilled. But for the most part, my children, and so many like them, come to school ready to absorb lessons and comply with authority so that they can move on with their lives. As long as the school doesn't mess that up, it's all good.

For too many other students, however, what my children have experienced isn't good enough. They need much more than caretaking and maintenance of the status quo. For many students of color, poor students, English language learners, and students with special needs, school is the difference maker. For them, great educators make all the difference. Highly skilled educators are required if we want our most vulnerable students to meet the same standards that my children have little problem achieving. Students who aren't "just-add-water" need a school where a great leader brings everything together to create a culture of excellence and an array of opportunities for them to thrive. Such effort takes more than goodwill and passion; it must be cultivated, nurtured, and sustained. System leaders, in fact, can be the key driver of creating schools where all students can succeed, through a deliberate focus on how the people within them are managed and led.

The evidence is clear that teaching matters when it comes to helping students achieve standards.[3] But great teaching doesn't just happen. School leaders have a significant effect on creating the conditions for great teaching by being both instructional leaders and effective managers.[4] System leaders, then, have a moral imperative to ensure that the students who need great educators get them. Teachers don't all come to their positions prepared to meet the incredible demands of educating diverse sets of students. In fact, education preparation programs do only part of the job. Richard Elmore used to say that education is the only sector with a "zero percent depreciation" model. He decried a paradigm that assumes teachers come into schools with one hundred percent of the knowledge and skills they need to succeed, which then decreases over time. Other industries operate under the opposite assumption, like that of my first principal, Judy; new employees know little and it's up to leaders to help them develop the skills and knowledge needed to succeed. Moreover, in many districts with the most vulnerable students, teachers come in with less preparation than their peers in wealthier districts—and the most vulnerable students are much more likely to be assigned a poorly prepared teacher than those in wealthier districts.[5]

When I became superintendent in Montgomery County Public Schools (MCPS), I was struck by the deep commitment to teacher development.

The system had a long-standing approach to developing new teachers and addressing poor performance of any teacher—tenured or not—through "consulting teachers." These teachers worked on a three-year rotation. They supported new colleagues who were learning the job, while also coaching those whose performance had been deemed ineffective through the evaluation and peer-assistance review (PAR) process. Any teacher, tenured or not, could be placed into PAR after a principal's evaluation was submitted to a panel of administrators and teachers who deemed the review to be credible. A consulting teacher was then assigned to work with that teacher to help them improve. If the teacher improved after a year, they were out of PAR. If not, they remained in for another year or left the district.

The MCPS PAR program was considered the gold-standard evaluation and review process in the country. It was the result of shared values, collaborative decision-making, and a commitment to excellence and equity. Part of the beauty of PAR was how it strengthened equity throughout the system. When the Montgomery County Educators Association (MCEA) proposed it in the late 1990s, the demographics of the school system were rapidly changing. MCEA leadership had a deep commitment to meeting the needs of all students and wanted to ensure that standards for teachers reflected the expectation that they would teach in an equitable manner. One small example of this practice is the use of "equity sticks." Rather than pose a question and then call on the child who raises their hand, teachers would have a cup of popsicle sticks with each child's name and then randomly draw one from the cup. This small practice mitigates the tendency that many teachers have to call on the same children who constantly raise their hands, while perhaps trying to coax an answer out of another, more reticent student. These "equity sticks" are a simple yet powerful tool to take the teacher's preconceived notions about who's more likely to have the right answer out of their hands and make teaching truly objective. It is also one of many easily observable practices that a teacher can be evaluated on as a leading indicator of their performance.

MCPS dedicated a lot of resources to supporting teachers as they acquired these kinds of practices. It was a clear expectation, there was professional development to learn how to engage all children, and equity was a standard in the evaluation process. So, when a teacher was evaluated, their equity stance and commensurate practices were part of the determination as to whether they deserved tenure or continued employment. If the teacher was placed in PAR, it was their peers who helped correct and adjust their practice, not administration. The end result was that this process, while expensive and time-consuming, was an allocation of resources, collectively decided, that reinforced the system's values. And teacher practice improved, which led to increased student learning and achievement for all children.

Another serious equity consideration regarding talent management has to do with teacher diversity. Teachers of color are far and few between; approximately 80 percent of teachers are white, with 77 percent being white female, although younger teachers are more diverse than ever.[6] Districts are working hard to diversify the profession, as are outside groups, such as Educators Rising, which is a Phi Delta Kappa (PDK) program. Research has emerged over the last few years showing the impact of teachers of color on student achievement,[7] and it's also simply the right thing to do. Yet teachers of color tend to leave their schools and the profession at a greater rate than white teachers.[8] Reasons for leaving are often tied to them not feeling valued, not having access to leadership opportunities, being expected to explain issues of racism to their colleagues, or disagreeing with the values of the school.[9] System leaders trying to drive a transformation agenda through an equity lens, then, have a responsibility to consider how they are attending to the needs of an increasingly diverse group of educators. One way to do so is through the establishment of affinity groups. I first saw the power of creating such entities when I was superintendent of Stamford and worked with leaders at GE, who has them for a multitude of employee groups. In MCPS a group of Black male educators started the BOND project when I was there, which is now a national model for creating supportive spaces for teachers whose identities don't reflect the district's majority.

When everyone is treated the same, it can be hard to differentiate supports to certain categories of employees. Judy, my first principal, found a way to do so, but too many school leaders don't. System leaders, then, have to find ways to help principals manage their talent. System leaders can review data to compare retention rates among schools. Exit interviews can be held to see if there are any patterns or red flags when teachers of color leave. Recruiting and hiring practices can be reviewed to be culturally proficient. Data regarding promotions and leadership opportunities can be analyzed to determine whether employees of color have the same access as their white peers. All of these measures can make the system more culturally proficient and drive a transformational equity agenda.

Talent management is all about having a holistic view of who should be brought into the organization and how they should be developed, held accountable, and distributed (as discussed in Chapter 4). A comprehensive process starts with recruiting and hiring and extends to the organization of collective learning and opportunities for leadership and differentiation.

BEGIN AT THE BEGINNING

I didn't think a lot about recruitment and hiring processes when I first became a superintendent. That was handled by the Human Resources department. While I renamed that office in Stamford to be Human Capital Development, I was focused more on what do to with educators once we got them in the door than how to find the right people to come work for us. The teacher shortage wasn't as acute back then, so perhaps I didn't need to focus on the issue. More likely, it just wasn't on my radar screen because I had never been taught about its importance. I see it quite differently these days, given my current work with Educators Rising, as well as the increased focus on diversifying the profession. Finding the right people and convincing them to work for your organization should be at the top of the list of what system leaders do. Simply going to hiring fairs at the local university won't cut it anymore. Instead, leaders need a deliberate approach to recruiting the right people through partnerships with institutes of higher education (IHEs), choosing the right people to represent the system, and being transparent about what you stand for.

Approximately three-quarters of teachers go through traditional educator preparation programs, although urban districts and those with many poor students tend to hire more alternatively certified teachers.[10] Programs like Teach for America may have captured the public's imagination while legislators throughout the country push for an increase in alternative certification, but system leaders largely go to their local and regional IHEs to recruit candidates. The rules of how they do so, however, should be subject for debate, as few superintendents collaborate with local IHEs on aligning standards and establishing grow your own (GYO) programs, incentives, and nontraditional pathways.

Leaders who are driving an equity-based transformation agenda must have a distinct view of what great teaching and learning looks like. As discussed in Chapter 1, a transformational equity agenda starts with content. What do young people need to know and be able to do in order to achieve standards, and what knowledge and skills do adults need to help them get there? Superintendents should work with the dean of the local educator preparation program to align their program with the expectations of the school system they'll likely work for. While the IHE may not see themselves as a workforce development arm of the district, the process itself can result in collective learning on both sides. School district leaders can increase access to a knowledge base grounded in research that can influence how they develop teachers and support students. University faculty can get a richer perspective of the impact and utility of their work and adjust accordingly.

IHEs also have self-interest to motivate them to work more closely with school districts as there's been a 35 percent decline in enrollment in educator preparation programs (EPPs) nationally over about ten years.[11] To boost enrollment, they must consider GYO programs that start in high school or that encourage current employees to pursue a teaching degree. But simply exposing them isn't enough. IHEs can provide incentives for students to continue this pathway while in college through dual enrollment agreements or by offering credit for course completion or earned microcredentials. Such programs help diversify the profession too, but it takes intentionality on the part of the district.

System leaders also often overlook another great resource sitting right in front of them: support professionals. Paraprofessionals, secretaries, bus drivers, custodians, and others are all potential teachers if someone just asked them. Many don't have the time, money, or academic background to enroll in a typical educator preparation program. And certainly, some of them aren't interested. Yet, leaders that see the people in those jobs as future teachers and organize to help them get on the path will not only open up another avenue for recruitment but will serve their communities by helping people get a higher paying job. When I was in MCPS I was struck by how the Service Employees International Union (SEIU), a local 500 association for support professionals helped their members advance, and many went on to become teachers. They knew it made their union stronger to have members working toward a future goal, and the district collaborated on a workforce development strategy. Local IHEs can and should be part of this solution by offering classes in the evening or online, giving credit for work experience and providing academic and financial supports. System leaders should be working with IHE leaders to create these kinds of programs, as it's to everyone's benefit.

This collaborative process already happens in some systems and is certainly not an innovative or disruptive approach. It's simply common sense, but also hard work. It requires that a team of system leaders builds a relationship and commits to collaborate with university faculty. Ideally, such an effort would be led by a cross-role team with representation from departments of curriculum, professional development, and human resources, as well as a principal and master teacher. Complete alignment can't be guaranteed, but this kind of process can at least ensure that the receiving end of the equation knows what to expect when they hire a new teacher.

FACE FORWARD

Partnerships with IHEs to develop the next generation of teachers, find homegrown talent, and align expectations are only part of the solution. Recruitment is another opportunity for leaders to rewrite the rules and reinforce the system's commitment to equity by considering both the language used to present the schools to a prospective candidate, and who is doing the talking. Young people today want to work for an organization that embraces diversity, is ethical, and cares about them.[12] As they peruse the tables at a hiring fair or go on a district's website, the system's values must be abundantly clear. It's a buyer's market these days, given the teacher shortage, and districts need a strategy for selling themselves to prospective employees. By trumpeting its values and beliefs, the district can better attract people who want to work in schools committed to equity.

In order to attract more diverse candidates, school systems should also use employees already in their midst to be recruiters. Candidates of color are more likely to want to work for a system that has people who look like them.[13] Leaders can use alumni networks to recruit, which should extend to the interview process, too. Any potential teacher needs to know that the school they're considering joining will value and support them. White leaders have a bigger hill to climb when it comes to convincing prospective teachers of color that this school will be different than others. They must be explicit about the system's values and structures that support employees of color. With a colleague of color leading the recruiting or interviewing process, potential candidates can see the manifestation of that commitment.

The interview process is all about values. The values of the candidate and those of the system are on display, either explicitly or implicitly. When I was interviewing to be superintendent of Stamford, the board asked me to give three reasons why there was an achievement gap. After the interview, the search consultant told me that my answer was one of the key differentiators that got me the job. Other candidates said things like, "No access to Pre-K," or, "Some parents don't value education." My response was, "Low expectations, low expectations, low expectations." I then, of course, explained that when adults don't have the belief system that all children can learn at a high level, and the skills and knowledge to support them, we'll continue to see achievement gaps. My values and beliefs were made abundantly clear; it's up to adults to figure out how to improve their practice in order to ensure all students have access to rigorous, high-quality instruction. Blaming students, families, and factors beyond the school system's control is simply excuse-making.

When I became superintendent, I used a similar question to flesh out someone's values and beliefs. I would only hire leaders who shared my commitment to equity. By asking the question, "Why do you think there's an achievement gap," you can quickly understand where an educator puts the locus of responsibility. Is it on the child or the system they're in? An equity lens demands attention to the latter. If someone doesn't already understand that, I don't want to have to work to convince them.

My other favorite interview question is, "Tell me about some adversity you've experienced and what you learned from it." Some people I've interviewed provide a personal example, while others stay in the professional domain. I've had some leaders cry while relating a childhood tragedy or personal difficulty that shaped them into the educator they've become. Others have stuck to a basic narrative about a professional challenge they faced. There's no right answer to this question, and it runs the risk of having candidates compete in the oppression Olympics. What it does, however, is flesh out whether the candidate has reflected, learned, and grown from their experiences. To lead and work for equity, you have to know yourself first. White people, in particular, have to focus within and understand their own story before they can effectively engage with colleagues and students of color. By asking this question in an interview, a leader can understand how much work the candidate still has to do.

Now That You've Got Them, How Will You Keep Them?

There is no mystery regarding what makes a great teacher. They have content expertise and a range of pedagogical skills. They engage all students while differentiating to provide support and acceleration. They assess students regularly so they can adjust instruction and get outside intervention if need be. They are facile with using the right technologies. They connect with their students and make sure each of them feels valued and respected within their learning community. They know how to address difficult issues of race, gender, and sexual orientation in respectful, sensitive, and productive ways. Great teachers work well with adults too, whether it's regularly communicating with families or collaborating with their peers.

The attributes of great teachers fill a long list. It's frankly a little crazy to expect any teacher to be the master of all of these components. Yet, every year, teachers are hired, given some preliminary training, assigned a group of young people, given the keys to their classroom and sent along their way. Good leaders understand Elmore's warning about the "zero percent depreciation model." They may assign a mentor teacher or even have something like the consulting teacher in MCPS. But the system itself is organized to assume that teachers pretty much know what they're doing and that the learning should be done by students.

Many other countries don't organize their talent this way. Critics of American public schools love to compare our results to those of other countries, yet they conveniently leave out the significant differences in the actual job of being a teacher. Not only is pay higher in other countries, many teachers spend less time instructing students and more time learning with peers. In some nations, teachers have responsibilities to mentor others, lead learning, and even conduct research on issues within the school.[14] Time is spent creating the conditions for success for adults to do their best work, which then leads to them serving children at a high level. In the United States, there is little incentive to focus on the needs of adults (remember Children First?), as the politics and rhetoric is all about the students. Some of this dynamic may be related to the fact that teaching is a largely female profession controlled by men.[15] It could be due to anti-unionism, or perhaps the general lack of faith and confidence Americans have in institutions.[16] Regardless, it's left school system leaders with a very large hill to climb if they want to rewrite the rules of how talent is organized to learn so that their practice improves and children are served at a higher level. System leaders can rewrite the rules by focusing on collective learning, principal supervision, and strategic staffing.

Organizing for Collective Learning

We don't have a student learning problem in America, we have an adult learning problem. Young people know how to learn. In fact, they're always learning, regardless of what they're being taught. Adults are the ones who need to regularly learn new skills, content, and technologies in order to engage students and meet their needs. But collective learning is not just an essential tool for people to develop necessary practices, it's also a management strategy to keep adults engaged and satisfied in their work. Adults who feel engaged in their place of employment are more productive and more likely to stay with that organization.[17] Retaining good teachers, especially teachers of color, can be a challenge, especially in schools serving a large number of vulnerable students,[18] which is why system leaders need to review retention rates by demographics every year and incorporate that metric into principal evaluations. Leadership, therefore, is about organizing effective structures and processes for adults to learn.

There's also a financial incentive to retaining teachers by engaging them in collective learning. People comprise more than 80 percent of district budgets. To succeed, they need differentiated supervision and supports, and our children clearly need their educators to be at the top of their game. Improvement requires investments. It always infuriated me when I would present my budget to elected officials who questioned why we needed more professional learning for educators. They assumed teachers already knew what to do. Inadequate student achievement was blamed on the students themselves, families, culture, a bloated central office, or a teacher's simple laziness. This latter notion—that educators have all of the skill, but not the will—was the basis of much of the reform movement of the last twenty years. Movies like *Waiting for Superman* demonize teachers and their unions to promote market-based reforms. Policies with no valid basis in evidence and based on incorrect assumptions that perpetuate the wrong approaches to improving teacher practice have been pushed through state legislatures. More problematic, federal programs like Title I are often used to purchase more new programs, curriculum, and technology rather than invested in the actual practices that help adults improve. And politicians don't want to hear that you can't simply quickly buy or legislate your way out of problems with a new policy or the purchase of a new program. Public education loves shiny objects, but collective learning is the only brass ring to grab on the carousel of improving educator practice.

System leaders, then, have a responsibility to help schools manage talent for collective learning. At the school level, principals must distribute leadership so that they're not the only ones leading the learning. Through strategic staffing and scheduling decisions, principal supervisors can help school leaders organize effective professional learning communities. Then, they must review the actual content of those PLCs and its impact on teacher practice. There's a through line from the school's vision and need, to the information that's used to inform the intended change, to the preferred adult practice that will help students learn more and better, to the way a teacher learns that practice, to the ongoing support, adjustment, and ultimate evaluation of whether they achieved the expected result. There must be intentionality to how a leader organizes all of those processes so that adults are learning new knowledge and skills. It's not fair to simply ask teachers to take on new work without providing the structure for them to do it. Richard Elmore calls this responsibility "reciprocal accountability": I can't hold you accountable for doing something that you don't know how to do. Therefore, I must help you develop the expected knowledge and skills and guide and support your change in practice before I hold you accountable for meeting the standard.[19]

A key responsibility of system leaders who supervise principals is to serve as buffers between schools and other central office departments. The list is long of professional development that is either required or deemed necessary by a central office program administrator. The state may have a new regulation about a minimum number of hours of training in a certain area that every teacher must have. The board of education may have adopted a new curriculum or program that requires outside experts to come in for a period of time and teach the new stuff. Student achievement data may have raised alarm bells and spurred a flurry of activity to quickly intervene, requiring that teachers do something different with a particular group of students. Many of these may have some legitimacy, and none can be fully avoided. Yet, if we know that adults learn best when engaged in authentic learning with their peers, they're not likely to change their practice when something is solely imposed from on high. The principal supervisor has to work with both their colleagues in central office and school leaders to strike the right balance between mandated professional development and authentic, collaborative professional learning.

Distributing leadership for collective learning within a school also provides opportunities to develop the next generation of leaders. Not all leadership in schools is formally designated and given a title, as positions and salaries need to be negotiated and everyone within a bargaining unit is treated the same. They may prefer a leadership position that is not administrative and want to keep one foot in the classroom working with students, or coach their peers, or write curriculum or develop a new program. Employees that want these opportunities but can't find them won't be as engaged and may leave. This has a direct cost and negative effect on the system. System leaders should be negotiating with bargaining units, if necessary, to create formal career ladders for teachers to lead within their schools and the district.

Primacy of the Principal

The literature is rife with improvement processes for induction, onboarding, mentoring, support, professional learning, placement, evaluation, leadership opportunities, and career advancement. All of those areas must be attended to when trying to improve schools. None of them on their own are worth much; a superintendent needs to see them holistically. Recruiting great candidates doesn't mean they'll stay if they work in a school that doesn't support them, which is yet another reason to conduct exit surveys and analyze retention data. The glue that holds all of these elements together is the principal. Which means, that once again, we're back to principal supervision.

Supporting principals requires differentiation. Some principals are in "first do no harm," schools and may need a relatively light touch organizing a long-term plan for improving adult practice. Other principals are in schools with a solid foundation that still have a long way to go to meet the needs of all of their children. Still others may be in a turnaround situation where swift and bold action is required in order to begin improvement. Mixed in with all of this is the experience level of the principals and the knowledge and skills of their supervisors. Superintendents, then, have to fit all of the pieces together to manage the talent in front of them so that educators are thriving in schools that support their development and growth. Superintendents need to rewrite the rules of how principals are supported in their management of talent. There are two main areas that leaders need to organize collaborative central office work-around: the effective use of data and a differentiated approach according to student needs. But all of this, as will be described further in Chapter 6, must happen within a culture of trust, both within the school and between the school and central office.

BRING THE DATA

According to Elizabeth Arons, head of the Urban Schools Human Capital Academy, one of the primary responsibilities of a human resource leader is to bring the data. Elizabeth knows of what she speaks, having been the head of human resources in Fairfax, Virginia; Montgomery County, Maryland; and New York City. Since 2010, her nonprofit has helped districts throughout the country improve their approach to human resources. All of Elizabeth's work has centered on helping system leaders help principals, especially those who lead schools with the most vulnerable students. According to Elizabeth, the best human resource leaders work with principal supervisors in a deliberate and intentional way grounded in multiple forms of data.

I inherited Elizabeth's leadership when I went to Montgomery County. While she had left a few years before I got there, some of the systems she put in place were baked into the DNA of the organization. I still remember my first spring staffing meeting. All the principal supervisors sat in a conference room with the human resources team. One by one, they discussed every administrator in the 202 schools and those in the leadership development program. Their strengths and needs were presented by those who knew them best and had observed them throughout the year, and then their placement for the next year was determined. Observational data was brought to bear on the critical decision of who gets to lead.

According to Elizabeth, the most effective human resource and principal supervisor tandems sit with a principal to go through their staff roster a couple of times per year and review the performance of each employee. Then, they can help the principal manage their talent. Perhaps one teacher needs to improve significantly, which will likely involve the union, so the human resources leader can start lining up the process. Maybe certain teachers haven't been effective at integrating the new equity training, and the principal supervisor has to talk to the district equity team to get them more support. Most importantly, knowing who is likely to retire or leave and what kind of teacher the principal wants to replace them allows the human resource leader to get an early start on recruiting and finding the right fit for the school. This kind of work requires the establishment of routines, clear expectations, and comprehensive information to make good decisions.

Managing talent also requires that leaders build a system of differentiation that takes the range of performance into account. In a system with all "first do no harm" schools, this may not be as important as in one that is more diverse. In the latter case, leaders have to rewrite the rules of how people are placed and supported within schools. When I was in Montgomery County, I recognized the need to help one of our high schools make dramatic changes. It had the most students on free and reduced price meals in the county and was the least desirable magnet program. As the building was scheduled to be razed, I saw an opportunity. If a brand-new building was going to be built, there would likely be questions about the instructional program. Why was the performance and enrollment lower than other high schools, and what were we going to do about it? It was a perfect chance for me to spur some real school improvement. I did so by setting up an advisory group of internal and external stakeholders and allocating money in the budget to bring in experts in project-based learning, as that was the instructional approach for the school. I assigned central office curriculum leaders to work with the school. I also insisted that it be a teacher-led initiative that activated student voice in the design process.

Most importantly, however, was the agreement of the MCEA to zero-base the school's staff. Doug Prouty, the head of the union at the time and a fierce equity warrior who's as smart as they come, knew that in order for the school to succeed it had to have the right staff. He allowed us to tell every teacher that they had to reapply for their position. And he made sure they couldn't be involuntarily transferred. So, if a teacher didn't want to work in the new program, they could go to another school of their choice that had an opening. Because I had a great relationship with Doug and he saw the authenticity of the teacher-led work that was happening at the school, he didn't want the old rules to stand in the way. The data presented a clear and compelling case for change, and the union and I agreed that we would differentiate our approach. We rewrote the rules of talent management to improve conditions for students.

According to Elizabeth, the best systems take this kind of differentiated approach to managing talent. Some teachers should be paid more for certain responsibilities. Some schools need more support than others. And sometimes principals should be allowed to skirt the regulations in order to do the right thing. An example of this is the requirement in some districts that a principal interview three candidates before making a hiring decision. At face value, this may make sense, especially if you want a diverse teaching staff and you want to control for bias. But, if the principal knows who they want—perhaps it's a student teacher who worked with them for the year, or a colleague in another school—why shouldn't they be allowed to hire them without wasting time interviewing others? If there's a concern that the principal isn't hiring a diverse pool of candidates, a principal supervisor can control for that by looking at hiring, promotion, evaluation, and retention data. Rather than try to manage everything up front, the human resource leader and principal supervisor can review that data as part of the principal's evaluation, which is much more effective than simply front-loading the process.

NAME, STRENGTH, AND NEED

Susan Enfield has been superintendent of Highline, Washington, since 2012. After leadership positions in the region, including Seattle, she came to Highline because the system was ready for her kind of leadership. A diverse district of nearly 20,000 students in thirty-three schools, the system had already embarked on an equity journey prior to her arrival. Susan was looking for a place to lead an equity-based transformation agenda, and Highline fit the bill perfectly. A major element of Susan's approach has been changing how system leaders manage talent. Working with Meredith Honig, an expert from the University of Washington, Highline has strategically aligned the work of Chief Academic Officer Susanne Jerde and Chief Talent Officer Steve Grubb. Through their collaboration and a deliberate focus on managing people within a complex ecosystem, the system has seen significant improvement.

Before even starting in Highline, new teachers know what they're getting into. Susan has increased the number of teachers of color through a concerted effort that puts their values on their sleeves as they recruit. Perhaps because she's a former English and journalism teacher, and a master communicator, she knows the power of language. According to Susan, by being intentional about their values around equity and belief that every child must be known by "name, strength and need," they've been able to find the kind of people they want to work in their schools. Once in the system, they become part of a community of equity-minded educators dedicated to improving their practice. Steve has instituted processes to ensure that hiring practices are flexible and aligned to the needs of the individual schools. Based on solid projections and conversations with principals about needs, they hire early to get the right kind of people. Susan has also worked with local IHEs to make sure they know what she's looking for and what teachers can expect when they come to Highline.

Susan is a big believer in finding the right people and giving them leeway to innovate and succeed. Over nine years she's built a powerful team,
anchored by Susanne and Steve. The two of them have worked together
to ensure that principals get regular, ongoing support, grounded in data.
They have shifted the roles of central office staff to support schools, which
has meant that system leaders have had to learn new skills and practices.
They've changed the strategic planning process to take a longer view, which
provides more stability, but coupled it with more frequent support from
supervisors so that principals can react quickly to changing conditions.
By decreasing the ratio of principal supervisors to principals, they've been
able to offer the kind of differentiated supports, based on comprehensive
data, that schools need. Principal supervisors work in six-week inquiry cy-
cles with their schools and bring their learnings back to the central office
teaching and learning team. That team then determines whether an individual principal needs additional support or if there's a systemic issue that
needs to be addressed. They're engaged in constant inquiry and reflection
about whether adult actions are aligned to the clear and nonnegotiable
goals Susan has established for Highline.

Susan and her team have operationalized what I believe is one of the
most important leadership qualities: slow down the inquiry to speed up
the action. She did that when she first began in Highline as she carefully
considered the kind of team she needed. Susan got to know people before
making judgements about their capacity. This approach extended to how
she overhauled her high schools. Despite glaring inequities, which manifested in having more advanced courses in schools with more affluent students, Susan knew she needed to take time to build a coalition of people
who supported the changes and could actually make them happen. I took
the same approach in Stamford when detracking the schools. It's easy to
just pick a fight and enact policy changes. It's much harder but ultimately
more effective to work with people to embrace a new approach.

Susan is the first to acknowledges that the work isn't done. In addition
to their research partner, Meredith Honig, Susan has the cabinet work with
an executive coach. They're constantly focused on both what they need
to get done and how they're working together. Early on, Susan realized
that cabinet members needed to get to know each other's work in order to

start collaborating in support of schools. Through their regular attention to their own practice they've come to realize that they're taking on too many tasks and not leading strategically. To my mind, this recognition is critical for any leader. As I ask my team all the time, what's the work that only you can do? If you're doing someone else's work then you're not fulfilling your responsibilities, which doesn't serve the organization. This kind of constant reflection and readjustment are essential components of effective teams, and Susan Enfield has certainly built one.

CONCLUSION

Susan Enfield's leadership is all about creating the right culture for people to do their best work. Leadership is about articulating a vision, establishing a mission, being crystal clear about how you expect people to achieve that mission, finding people who can meet your expectations, and then creating the conditions for success. How people interact every day within that framework is culture. Leaders like Susan both model the kind of culture they want and ensure that the people around them will do the same. In Chapter 6, I'll describe how system leaders can improve and create powerful cultures that support an equity-based transformation agenda.

System improvement and school improvement happen through and with people. What adults do with each other and with children every day determines the success or failure of an equity-based transformation effort. Leaders must establish processes for people to do their best work, as more than 80 percent of a district's budget is personnel. Moreover, the true test of leadership is the ability to help others be as effective as possible. School systems, after all, are about teaching and learning. That notion shouldn't stop with children. Adults, too, need to be constantly engaged in learning with and from each other how to best serve young people.

A running theme throughout this book has been the primacy of the principal. Successful talent management requires that principals are helped by central office leaders to navigate the complexity of organizing educators into professional learning communities, buffering from distractions, engendering accountability, and using multiple measures of data. Equally important are the processes by which districts ensure that the right people are coming to—and staying in—the system. System leaders are responsible for creating the conditions by which principals are supported in their efforts to align their people to the school's and district's vision and needs.

System leaders must also use comprehensive metrics and put in place support mechanisms to keep the right people in the system. Exit interviews, focus groups, surveys, and reviews of transfer and retention rates, can all help principals make better decisions and be accountable for their leadership in managing talent. All of these data should be disaggregated by demographics to determine if there are patterns that need to be addressed. Structures such as affinity groups can also be used to support educators. By creating these structures and taking a comprehensive look at data, superintendents send a powerful signal that they're looking out for the best interests of their people. And as we'll see in the next chapter, how people come together to address student needs and activate the vision of the district is the key ingredient in any equity-based transformation effort.

6

School System Culture: If It Walks Like a Duck and Talks Like a Duck...

WHEN I BECAME superintendent of Montgomery County, Maryland (MCPS), I embarked on a "listening and learning" tour as part of my entry into the district. MCPS was not in crisis; it did not need drastic turnaround. In fact, MCPS was widely considered the most successful large district in the country. Books and case studies had been written about its achievements under my predecessor, who had a twelve-year run. There was no denying the outcomes. The board and I knew I would have to ease into the position and get to know people and how the system worked before making change. My extensive visits to schools and communities, coupled with a transition team that analyzed strengths and needs, provided me the opportunity to understand the system.

It became apparent very quickly that I was leading an organization whose culture needed to change. Stakeholders were rightfully proud of how MCPS had addressed the requirements of No Child Left Behind (NCLB). But now it was the Common Core era. Standards had been raised, and measures of student progress were changing. Students and families with more significant needs had increased over the years. The economic boom of the first decade of the 2000s had ended with the Great Recession, and difficult budget decisions had to be made. Perhaps most germane to how I would lead the district was the fact that people were tired of the top-down approach that had both led to significant achievement and frustrated many stakeholders. There was no doubt that MCPS had experienced great success. But new challenges needed a fresh approach.

I remember saying to my board early on, "So you want me to ensure that more students, many of whom are more vulnerable than ever, achieve a higher standard, and do it with less money than we've had in a way that everyone feels good about." To which they said, essentially, yes. It was clear to me the district had smart people, comprehensive systems, a supportive community, and enough resources. What MCPS needed was a shift in how people interacted with each other around a shared vision and collective understanding of the new challenges. The district needed to address its culture, which became a central focus of my tenure. After all, it's the work that only the superintendent can do.

The superintendent of schools is the keeper of the system's culture. While they inherit an extant culture when taking the job, they can also change it. In fact, they're the only one who can fully do so. Superintendents seeking to transform a system through an equity lens must focus on both school culture and that of the overall system. For schools, a strong culture grounded in collective learning, shared ownership and accountability, collaborative decision-making, a love for children, and a belief in their unlimited potential is essential. Such schools can exist despite the larger context around them, and therein lies the rub. Given the paltry results of system-wide transformation efforts, if districts aren't going away, perhaps the culture of these entities also needs to be addressed. How change is driven throughout large, complex systems is part of why they're not succeeding. Closer attention to culture would enable a greater change. This chapter suggests ways to rewrite the rules of culture by proposing that leaders need to pay close attention to the unwritten rules of a system and then model the behavior they want to see. Previous chapters have described the major drivers of how leaders can transform systems through an equity lens. These levers that leaders can pull will only get them so far without a strong culture that forms the foundation of complex work.

The importance of school culture has been firmly established in the literature. Research has shown that how people interact within a school around a shared vision can be the difference maker.[1] Given the substantial evidence base, it's not necessary to make the argument that culture is a foundational factor in school improvement efforts. It's more important, in my view, for system leaders to understand their ability to influence how an improvement culture can be established and sustained to drive an equity agenda. They must also be clear about its meaning. Culture is how people interact with each other within a community. Bolman and Deal's description is one of my favorites:

> Culture is both a product and a process. As a product, it embodies accumulated wisdom from those who came before us. As a process, it is continually renewed and re-created as newcomers learn the old ways and eventually become teachers themselves.[2]

In schools and districts, like any organization, trust is the key element of an improvement culture. People need to know their colleagues and boss have their back. They must be able to take risks without the fear of being blamed if they make a mistake. They need to be public with their practice and vulnerable in order to learn, grow, and improve. They must be able to voice their opinions and perspectives without fear of alienation. They need to know that their values and beliefs are welcome. And they must trust that their performance will be judged fairly, and they'll have opportunities to grow based on merit. Yet, trust can be hard to garner, especially between central office leaders and schools.

As described in previous chapters, central office functions can be isolated and siloed. The people within distinct program and administration divisions can be competing for resources, time, and attention for their area of responsibility. Political demands, long-standing relationships, and different incentives can all hinder the development of trust within a central office. An example of this dynamic might be seen in the relationship among a principal supervisor and program administrators. A principal supervisor's success comes from the overall performance of schools relative to the district's accountability system. The success of a program administrator for special education (SPED) or English language learners (ELLs) may be narrowly focused on subsets of students, with commensurate legal and financial consequences. The school principal sits in the middle of these system leaders and may have their own view of how to best serve all students, including those with distinct needs. How, then, can each of these leaders trust that the others' interests are not in conflict with each other if their performance incentives are different? Certainly, their work should be comingled in an overall strategy to increase student learning and performance.

But that takes effort and time. It's easier for the program administrator to stay siloed and focus only on their population. The less alignment among these entities, the less trust exists that they're all working towards the same goal. Yet the investment required to build trust among these leaders often gets waylaid by immediate demands to address pressing issues.

The pressure leaders are under to make change can dictate the degree of trust among leaders and stakeholders. Leaders who are driving an equity-based transformation agenda must take time to build trust with internal and external stakeholders, especially if they're new to the system. It's hard to do in a high-pressure situation where systems are broken, performance has been lagging for too long, and the politics are divisive. Trust may be easier to come by in a district that is otherwise stable but has experienced changes in demographics or stagnant performance and needs a new approach to get to the next level of work. In the first situation, the mandate to quickly address urgent problems can result in a leader not taking time to build relationships with followers. They may not collaborate and build collective leadership as they're faced with pressure from the board and community to act on behalf of students. Yet, their failure to do so compromises their ability to actually transform the system. Herein lies a bit of a paradox. According to Smylie,

> Reform pressure, alone or in combination with pressure from other sources, may push districts away from organizational behaviors that promote improvement, such as experimentation, risk-taking, innovation, creative adaptation, and productive organizational learning—behaviors encouraged by some of the most promising improvement strategies described in this volume. Moreover, reform pressure may push districts toward behaviors that are antithetical to improvement. Indeed, it can trigger maladaptive tendencies and snowball in a vicious cycle toward organizational distress and failure.[3]

Stability in system leadership is one key to sustaining a transformation effort. Unfortunately, stability of the upper tier of leadership can be elusive in too many districts that need it most. According to Daly, Finnigan, and Liou's summary of the research, "About 15 percent to 33 percent of leader across a typical district vacate their positions each year."[4] According to them, such leaders build relationships within networks in the system that then lead to school improvement. The "churn" that happens when they leave can then disrupt those efforts. In their study of one large urban district, it tended to be the most effective system leaders who left, possibly because they were overburdened and underrecognized. Daly, Finnigan, and Liou suggest that one way to counteract such departures is to increase the level of trust within the system, which requires vulnerability and risktaking. Trust is the essential element of cultures that drives improvement. Superintendents, therefore, have to rewrite the rules of culture by paying close attention to the dynamics within their system that may be causing good people to leave, and they have to act as a buffer from political forces that may cause undue pressure.

THE INTERSECTION OF EQUITY AND CULTURE

Leaders who seek to drive an equity agenda face a complex task when trying to change culture. Competing interests among stakeholder groups can be deeply entrenched, and their political powers are imbalanced. Their locations on the continuum of outrage and apathy must also be considered, as some stakeholders are deeply involved in either trying to change the system or maintain the status quo, while others have resigned themselves to just go along to get along. Moreover, as school districts are American constructs, they're subject to all of the polarization and identity politics that have torn us apart over the years. And the institutional racism of so many of our institutions (housing, policing, finance, health care) forms the foundation for their view of, and access to, the levers of power that accelerate or thwart change. A leader who's trying to transform their system through an equity lens and understands the power of culture needs a strategy to address these intersecting dynamics.

As this book is about systems leadership, culture needs to be considered as a force that emanates both internally and externally. By internally I mean both within the central office and in the relationships to schools. By externally I mean the relationship to the community and formal and informal entities that have power. An equity agenda requires hard choices. It means that adult practice must change and the rules that have privileged few and oppressed many for years have to be rewritten. To lead for equity means making people feel uncomfortable, even as you're trying to bring them together and embrace a vision for a better future. It's incredibly hard work, rife with opportunities to fail. The easiest part of setting an equity agenda is the public pronouncement of the moral imperative to transform the system. The hardest part is the actual realignment of the way the system works so that the most vulnerable students are better served. That requires system leaders to use their formal and informal power to both get internal stakeholders to do something different every day with students, and inspire external stakeholders to embrace, or at least accept, that change. Superintendents must be cognizant of the regular, ongoing interactions among people around the complexity of the transformation effort, as that will spell its success or its doom.

Control or Influence?

Superintendents can't control everything, even though many stakeholders think otherwise. An essential leadership skill is to know what you can control and what you can influence. When it comes to sustaining an improvement culture, a superintendent should be sure to control what they have clear authority over while working to influence what they don't. Trust is built from clarity and transparency regarding these dynamics. Superintendents have complete control over the work of their central offices and must do whatever it takes to ensure its work is collaborative and cohesive. They have a significant degree of control over the relationship with employee associations and must use every tool they have to negotiate equity-minded contracts and exercise every clause therein to improve adult practice. Superintendents have little control over school cultures, but they can influence them through modelling behavior and principal supervision. More importantly, they can invest in understanding a school's culture so that they know the barriers and accelerants to driving an equity agenda. As I describe below, this latter leadership move is not only essential to transformation, it also provides personal satisfaction.

Interactions among leaders within the central office will effect a transformation agenda. Superintendents must organize the system around a set of clear, nonnegotiable goals, with accountability for system leaders. They must ensure collaboration and cohesion among the offices so that messages and supports to schools are coherent, focused, and aligned to the school's actual needs. To do this, the first question that must be asked is, "What's the problem we're trying to solve?" Each member of the leadership team may have a different view of the issue at hand, depending on their responsibilities. When a new technology is being rolled out, the curriculum leader may see it as an opportunity to deliver new content and quickly assess student learning. The data and research leader may see it as a way to gather new information that can help inform instructional decisions and strategy. The technology leader may view the solution as an opportunity to get teachers and students more comfortable with new technologies. None of them are wrong. Yet, unless the superintendent slows down the inquiry to ensure that everyone is on the same page, mixed messages might be sent to schools about the value of new technology. When communications aren't clear, confusion can take hold in a school, which breeds distrust and affects culture. Technology is relatively easy. Equity is much harder and requires even more coordination.

As I've written about in previous chapters, unions can be a force for good in schools, but they can also work against change. Regardless, they must be managed. The propensity to treat employees the same regardless of performance is both a management and cultural challenge. While due process is important so that the rights of employees aren't trampled, it can also hinder the ability of a school leader to address poor performance. When poor performance isn't quickly dealt with, others know it and see it. Their motivation to change and embrace a new direction can then be quashed by their observations of how a leader handles colleagues who aren't up to snuff. It comes down to, "Why should I take on new challenges and work harder if those around me can just do the same old thing with no consequences?"

System leaders, then, must help principals address employees who aren't pulling their weight. Principal supervisors can work with their colleagues in human resources to ensure they understand exactly which teachers need additional attention—whether to improve their practice (the best option) or evaluate them out (the option of last resort). Certified central office program staff can then be assigned to schools to support a principal in the evaluation process. Since great teachers are the number one equity lever, there is nothing more important than ensuring every child has one. This means that no administrative function should take precedent over addressing what happens in classrooms every day. Hence, if the literacy administrator needs to spend a certain number of days in schools assessing the effectiveness of a teacher's performance, so be it. Not only will the teacher's performance be addressed, but it also sends a strong signal to everyone about the seriousness of the superintendent's agenda. Culture is established through prioritization. If the superintendent assigns central office personnel to evaluate teachers, the message is sent that what happens in schools is the most important thing in a system, poor performance won't be tolerated, principals need support, and the top leader will do whatever it takes to make change happen.

The extant culture of schools is another challenge superintendents face, especially if they're new to the district. When I was a superintendent people would sometimes refer to me as the captain of the ship. I would respond that I was more like the admiral of a fleet, having to guide numerous boats of various sizes and speeds on a shared mission. In this metaphor, culture is an iceberg. People can see what happens at the top, when churning water hits against its side, like the big changes that get covered by local media and prompt outraged people to attend a board meeting. But what happens within schools among people every day is the thicker, unseen, and potentially more dangerous base. The superintendent who's guiding ships around the iceberg must work hard to avoid these perils and understand their power if they hope to transform the system.

Schools are full of "we-be's"—the people in the system who say, "We've been here long before you got here, and we'll be here long after you're gone." Unless it's a brand-new school with new leadership and staff, schools have served generations of families and have long-term employees with formal and informal responsibilities. While there's understandably a lot of recent focus on the teacher shortage and retaining teachers, we don't speak as often about the number of people that stay. Among the demands of parents, the beliefs and actions of employees and the stance of leadership, a culture exists that can accelerate or hinder an equity agenda. System leaders must carefully navigate its complexity. The best way to do so is to visit.

Getting a "Kid Fix"

The simplest way for a superintendent to understand a school's culture is to visit, often. Superintendents have multiple demands on their time and too many excuses to not visit schools. Moreover, they have staff whose job it is to be in schools. Yet nothing will give as much insight into a school's culture and ability to adopt an equity agenda as getting to know the people within it. When I first got to Montgomery County, I made it a point to visit every one of my 202 schools within the first two years. I did this partially to differentiate myself from the previous superintendent, and largely because I needed a regular "kid fix." My predecessor rarely visited schools, and when he did it was a big event. Principals would put out coffee and pastries, and folders with the school improvement plan would be spread on the table, as he would spend most of his time in the office. When I got there and realized that people were nervous to have me in the building, I would immediately thank them for the spread and ask the principal to start walking with me. As we walked the building, I introduced myself to every employee I met, insisting on saying hello to support staff. I would ask the principal open-ended questions as we walked, such as, "Tell me about your biggest challenge," or, "What are you most proud of in your school?" These kinds of questions would get them talking, and I could tell within thirty seconds whether the principal had an equity mindset and an instructional vision. I could also tell which ones were disingenuous. I would then enter classrooms to talk with teachers and students, as long as it didn't interrupt lessons. In a secondary school, during the change in classes I would make sure to stand in the hallways to see how students and adults interacted, and whether adults were standing in their doorways greeting students as they entered.

I also borrowed Carl Cohn's "Cookies with Carl" (more on this below) when I was a superintendent, both in Stamford and MCPS. At least once per year I would visit a school, lay out cookies and coffee, and have open conversation with employees with no administration present. They would ask me questions, I would share information, and most importantly, I would hear how they talked about students and families. These conversations, much like the open-ended questions I asked principals, would tell me almost everything I needed to know about the school's culture. Where did adults locate the needed change that would increase student learning? Did they blame students, or did they embrace the need to change their practice? How did they talk about issues of equity and different kinds of students? Would they criticize school leadership and complain about directives from central office, or did they offer useful feedback and insight on a new initiative? These visits were instrumental in helping me understand how far we'd have to travel on the ocean of equity.

Engaging students and parents also gives a leader great insight into the culture of a school. Town halls and focus groups show how young people feel about the adults around them. They also help a system leader understand the dreams and hopes of the next generation. Parents don't hold back and will tell a superintendent what they need to hear about whether their children are well taken care of. And, while it's often those who have the most to complain about who speak the loudest, patterns can be discerned when some things are repeated by multiple stakeholders.

None of these efforts to understand a school's culture stand on their own. Leaders have to triangulate the data and get a full picture of a school's readiness to embrace an equity agenda. But culture manifests in language. How something is described says a lot about the values and beliefs of the speaker and how they feel about the work before them. That feeling is grounded in their own view of whether they'll be able to meet challenges within their context. That context is defined by the people within it and how they interact on daily basis.

The other benefit of visiting schools regularly and talking with staff, students, and families in an open-ended way is that stakeholders can see what a leader values, which can help shift the culture. When the leaders of the support professionals association in Montgomery County told me they had heard from members that I made a point of introducing myself to secretaries, custodians, and cafeteria workers, they began to believe that I truly respected every employee in the system, a key tenet of our collaborative work together. When I visited a classroom and got down on the floor with students, and then posted a quick tweet after leaving the building about the great lesson I had just seen, teachers knew that I was paying attention to instruction and cared about teaching and learning above all else. When principals walked the halls with me and had an opportunity to share their stories, vision, and struggles, they knew that I was trying to get to really know them as leaders and people. And when families and students had the opportunity to talk with me about important issues, they knew that I had their backs and would have their needs at the top of mind when I was making decisions. By being in schools, leaders not only learn about the cultures that can make a transformation agenda sink or float, they're also modelling the kind of leadership that will transform schools, offices, and the whole system.

PROCESS IMPROVEMENTS

Superintendents can't—and shouldn't—control everything. They can, however, insist that decisions are made and challenges are faced by focusing on processes that build trust. As described in other chapters, the work of leading systems improvement is too complex to lend itself to easy answers. No purchase of a program or technology, implementation of a new curriculum, allocation of an expenditure, or passage of a policy will lead to sustained school system change. A superintendent's job is to embrace that complexity and align the various aspects of the organization around a collective vision and a shared understanding of needs. Stakeholders must be constantly learning and engaged in inquiry in order to figure out what's working and what needs to change. But learning and asking questions is hard; it can be confrontational and challenge long standing perspectives and ways of doing business. A strong culture allows for that difficult work to occur.

To engender and sustain such a culture a few things need to be in place. First, goals and outcomes must be clearly established. Then, the system needs a theory of action about how those goals will be achieved. There must also be clarity about roles and responsibilities and agreed upon norms for decision-making. Finally, stakeholders must collaborate with each other in a respectful way that allows for multiple perspectives to be brought to bear on the issues. Respectful interactions don't mean that everyone plays "in the land of nice," as educators are wont to do. Rather, they need to be critical friends and push each other to have honest conversations about the work.

Clear goals and outcomes are important aspects of culture because they reduce confusion among stakeholders. When people don't know what they're working toward, they may not be able to contribute their best effort, and they may not trust the work of others. It's important that goals and outcomes are established for both students and adults. When I was in Montgomery County, our strategic planning framework articulated what we wanted students to know and be able to and the adult actions that would lead to those goals. We established three broad focus areas for every school and department to focus on: academic excellence, creative problem solving, and social emotional learning. Corresponding each area were statements about what students and staff would do to achieve these goals. For example, under academic excellence, one of four expectations for students was to "demonstrate literacy across all content areas by reading complex texts, writing for multiple purposes, speaking in a variety of situations and using language effectively."[5] Commensurate statements for staff read that they will "differentiate instruction to meet the needs of all students," and "evaluate what students know and are able to do through multiple and diverse measures."[6] We then had academic and social-emotional learning measures to evaluate whether schools were on track. The language was intended to spark innovation and collective leadership rather than dictate what every one of the 202 schools would be doing every day. We established clear, nonnegotiable stakes in the ground with the expectation that school leaders would then lead their communities to take action to accomplish them.

Leaders also need a clear theory of action when driving an equity agenda. I remember first learning about theories of action as part of the Connecticut Center for School Change Superintendent's Network. In that group, Andrew Lachman and Richard Elmore convened about fifteen to twenty superintendents throughout the state in a process of collective observation, reflection, and learning. A superintendent would write a problem of practice, we would visit their district one month, then spend the next month discussing what we observed and how the superintendent could improve. As part of that work, we each had to write a theory of action about our own approach to change management. A theory of action is an "if/then" statement. If I do X, then Y will happen. When I came back with my first draft, I had written something like, "if adults are constantly engaged in collective inquiry, then they will learn the best practices to serve our students." While that statement reflected my core beliefs that adult learning was key, it was scant on details. My colleagues had written the opposite. Many of them presented what were essentially one-page plans with statements like,

> "If we have clear goals, and if we use the data to make decisions, and if we provide the right resources to teachers, and if we hold them accountable, and if we engage our families, and if we provide professional development, and if we have high standards for students, and if we have good curriculum, and if we regularly assess our students, then all students will achieve."

While my theory of action lacked specifics, I found those of my colleagues to be too much in the weeds and more tactical than strategic. I also learned that the words themselves are not the most important aspect of a theory of action. Much of its value lies in both the process of its construction and the articulation of a hypothesis. When done right, a theory of action can be a powerful collective enterprise that uncovers a community's values and beliefs about how change should happen. Teasing out those beliefs and understanding each other's stories and perspectives about why stakeholders think a distinct set of actions will lead to certain outcomes is a powerful culture-building exercise. The theory of action that I shared with my Connecticut colleagues may have served to clarify my own values and beliefs, but it did nothing to bring others into the process with me.

Theories of action can be sustainers of strong cultures because they're an articulated hypothesis that needs to be regularly tested. A statement about how one thinks change will happen does nothing on its own. Processes need to be put in place for collective data gathering, assessment, and adjustments if necessary. If you believe something will happen because of something else, you must test to see if it actually occurred in the way you thought it would. Did student learning increase because of the new curriculum that was adopted, or was it because of the professional learning needed to implement the curriculum and make adjustments? Perhaps the process of setting power standards prior to selecting a new curriculum caused teachers to better understand how to help students achieve. A theory of action that articulates collective action intended to lead to the desired change will help stakeholders understand why they're doing what they're doing. And the process of reflecting on it will enable them to make the necessary modifications and improvements along the way.

With clearly established goals for both students and adults and an agreed upon theory of action, leaders need to clarify roles and responsibilities and insist on norms for how people come together. Culture may seem elusive, but it can be developed and improved through clarity and specificity. As described in Chapter 3, decision-making processes are a big part of sustaining an improvement culture, as people like to know what to expect. Moreover, stakeholders want to know their roles in driving change. Sometimes their formal role might be different than the one they play as part of a collective leadership or learning group. Clarity around roles and responsibilities plays out in large ways and small. A member of a board of education might have the formal authority to approve a budget or pass a policy, but when they're at a community function, they can't address a stakeholder's complaint about a teacher. A principal has the authority to assign teachers to courses, but when they're in a school improvement team meeting, they may be just one voice amid those of faculty, staff, parents, and students. One way to establish clarity of roles and responsibilities and create norms for behavior is through the use of protocols.

All of us have been in meetings that feel pointless, long, and inefficient. We walk out of them with a deep sigh thinking that our time could've been better spent doing something—anything—else. In my experience the worst meetings are those that are least organized. Established protocols can help. Throughout my career I've used protocols from the National School Reform Faculty for almost any situation where people work together.[7] Protocols can be used to resolve conflict, discuss a piece of work, or reflect on a lesson. Whichever protocol is used, leaders need to establish the expectation that meetings will be organized with specific outcomes.

One of the most basic, yet powerful, protocols I learned from Larry Leverett in Plainfield, New Jersey, was how to build consensus. Since school systems are distinctly hierarchical places with clear lines of authority, it can be hard to establish a collaborative culture. In Plainfield we used a consensus process to make final decisions when working in LINCCs, the collaborative decision-making bodies comprised of various stakeholder groups.

At the end of the meeting, there was a consensus check. Rather than simply rely on everyone looking to the head of the table to see how Larry felt about the issue, each person would have to hold up a hand and show five or three fingers or a fist. Five fingers meant you were fully supportive of the decision. Three meant you could live with it and would publicly support it. A fist meant that you couldn't support the decision. The person who showed a fist then had to articulate the reasons why they couldn't support the decision. Then the group had to address that person's concerns to get them to move to at least three-finger support.

The idea behind this protocol is to get public support from every stakeholder and make sure that everyone has skin in the game and their views are represented. In too many meetings, people check out once they disagree. Then they walk to the parking lot with their colleague and complain, which often gets related to others outside of the meeting. A game of telephone ensues, and the decision has lost credibility before it even gets out of the gate. When a decision is made by consensus, no participant has that option. If they show a fist, they're required to voice their concerns, which the group then must address. Hence, they can't claim their voice wasn't heard. Moreover, the group benefits from hearing the views of various stakeholders, some of whom might not be willing to participate in a typical meeting that has the superintendent at the head of the table with a clear power differential. It's often the quietest voices who have the most to contribute when asked, which a consensus process can activate to the benefit of the group, the ultimate decision, and the system's culture.

Not all decisions should, or need to be, made by consensus. But here again, clarity is essential. There are times when a leader must make a decision and wants additional information. Other times they want consultation and input. And sometimes it's a collaborative decision. There's no clear rule as to which decision fits into which bucket, although collaboration is most useful when multiple stakeholders are affected by the decision. On the other hand, when driving an equity agenda, a superintendent often must make decisions that others won't necessarily like. In this case, going through a time-consuming collaborative decision-making process may water down the initiative or align too much to the politically powerful or loudest voices. Regardless of which tactic a leader uses, culture is established and sustained through clarity. It's incumbent upon the leader to say, "I've decided to open up access to advanced courses next year and I'd like some information about what the impact may be on students and teachers so we can plan accordingly." Or, they can say, "I'm thinking about opening up access to advanced courses next year and I'd like to consult with you about how to go about it and when." A leader can also say, "I'm wondering if opening up access to advanced courses is the right thing for us to do. I'd like us to collaborate on the decision before I bring it to the board." While I would lean toward the first or second approach, whichever one a leader takes, the clarity of the process is what establishes and sustains an improvement culture.

A DANGEROUS MAN

Someone once said that Carl Cohn is dangerous. When he told me this story, Carl couldn't recall who had made this statement. But he remembered that when he was superintendent in Long Beach, California, in the 1990s, as an "insider with an outsider's perspective," his views on how to transform the system of nearly one hundred thousand students were a departure from the old ways of doing business. Carl had grown up in Long Beach in the 1950s and 1960s, but went to Catholic school. He joined the seminary as a young man, then, inspired by Robert Kennedy, switched his passion to counseling, as he thought that would have a greater impact on his community. When he joined the Long Beach school system, he quickly distinguished himself as a young Black man who could work with people of all backgrounds. As Long Beach was experiencing significant gang-related tension and violence, that trait enabled him to rise through the ranks. Carl was asked to oversee the system's voluntary desegregation efforts in the 1970s due to his ability to bring a calming presence to any situation. Then he left for a four-year stint as an academic, first in Pittsburgh and then in Los Angeles before returning in 1988 to be an area superintendent and head of the district's antigang task force. In 1992, right after the Rodney King riots, Carl was appointed superintendent of schools. The system needed a calm, steady hand who was a known quantity, yet had the experience and perspective to bring much-needed stability to the system. For the next ten years, Carl Cohn would do just that by focusing on establishing a strong culture.

At the time, Carl took the helm of Long Beach the Rodney King riots and gang violence weren't the only dynamics in play. The state, like much of the country, was in the process of adopting new academic standards. This was also the era of zero tolerance, where behavioral transgressions would not be tolerated. So, Carl and the board developed a new slogan to signal their commitment to transformation: high standards for dress, behavior, and academics. Students were expected to achieve at a higher level, bad behavior wouldn't be tolerated, and a system-wide uniform policy was put in place to quell gang activity. Interestingly, this last move was embraced by the large and growing immigrant community, especially from Cambodia and Central and Latin America, where school uniforms were a signifier of elite schools. It also garnered national attention as a symbol of what needed to happen in urban systems throughout the country. Education Secretary Dick Riley visited and hailed the move, as did Attorney General Janet Reno and President Clinton, who mentioned it in one of his State of the Union speeches and then visited Long Beach. The district was clearly transforming. The question was how to get principals and employees to embrace the change.

Carl's work to shift the culture of Long Beach exemplifies one of my mantras; leaders need to do the work that only they can do. Carl intuitively recognized this and made sure that his work would be focused on finding the right talent, being highly visible in schools, and working closely with the board. Long Beach, like many systems, typically hired and promoted people from within. To become a leader, you had to go through the ranks, get to know the right people, and, according to Carl, "when you mellowed out by your mid-40s you were seen as ready to become a principal."

At Eva Baker's CRESST Center at UCLA, Carl found one of his key hires, a new head of research, Lynn Winters, a position that he elevated to cabinet level. Lynn brought a thoughtful, collaborative approach to her work. She spent a lot of time in schools, listening to and working with educators. One of her key moves that reinforced the culture Carl wanted to create was her response when teachers decried the new state standardized testing. Rather than just tell them they had to do it, Lynn worked with teachers to create new assessments that they felt were more reflective of the district's vision for teaching and learning. Carl and Lynn weren't going to negotiate whether all students should be reaching standards. Yet, they were willing to find a new, collective approach to get there. They were showing the people who were closest to the issues that they trusted them and were willing to find new ways to achieve collective goals. Moreover, Carl was showing other leaders in the system that he would empower them to do their best work while he focused on his.

People in the schools knew they could trust Carl because they had gotten to know him. Carl not only made a point of visiting schools, but he also established a regular routine of "cookies with Carl," where he would listen to teachers talk about their issues, hopes, and dreams. He also took groups of principals out to dinner on a regular basis so they could have open dialogue about what was happening throughout the system. Carl's counseling chops kicked into gear during these sessions with front-line educators, as anyone who's worked in the mental health field knows how to listen. Carl was doing the work that only he could do by being out in schools, engaging with educators, and showing how thoughtful he was while developing an understanding of their issues that he could then take back to his team. Culture was being strengthened through relationships and interactions.

None of Carl's leadership moves could have happened without a supportive board. He knew that superintendents tended to get anxious about their annual evaluations, and too many saw their boards as adversaries rather than partners. Carl decided to take a different tack and lean into the board work. He and the board met four times per year for two and a half days each time. For two days, they would discuss, in public, the overall strategy and direction of the district. The last half-day was a mini-evaluation of him, in executive session. By engaging with the board so often outside of the regular board meeting rituals and routines, Carl was building deep relationships and ensuring everyone was on the same page regarding the transformation of Long Beach. He was also showing the rest of the system that he was going to do the one job that only he could do. Superintendents need to buffer the rest of the system from the political dynamics. If they don't, other leaders throughout the system won't have confidence and trust that they'll be protected if they make a mistake, innovate in new ways, or ruffle feathers. Carl's work with the board not only gave them protection but offered them no excuse for doing their part to better serve the children of Long Beach.

Carl Cohn's emphasis on culture building was best symbolized by what he did, not what he said. One of the most powerful examples of this was his volunteering in a first-grade class in the toughest part of town. Carl went there on a regular basis and worked with children while developing a deeper understanding of what it meant to teach thirty first graders. He didn't have to do this; in a large and complex school system there are so many competing demands it can be hard to dedicate time to regularly being in a school. Yet Carl needed the "kid fix" of being with children and watching them grow, and he would also show everyone else that what happens in classrooms with children every day is more important than anything else. Moreover, since Carl didn't have an instructional background and wasn't an expert who was going in to show the teacher how to do it; he was modelling a learning stance. If the superintendent can be vulnerable and spend time learning how to help a teacher get children to read, then there's no excuse for anyone else to not change their own practice.

Carl Cohn's commitment to social justice was first found in faith, then, inspired by Bobby Kennedy, manifest in counseling. Those perspectives enabled him to couple his urgent passion to change outcomes and conditions for children with a deep empathy for the people doing the work. He knew that transformation takes time and that the people within the system had to embrace a new way of doing business rather than just be directed to change. By focusing on the work that only he could do, Carl created and sustained a culture over ten years that strengthened the practice of leaders and educators throughout the system. When it came time for him to leave, one of the young principals Carl had hired, Chris Steinhauser, who was now his deputy, became superintendent for the next eighteen years and built on that culture to create new and innovative approaches to teaching and learning throughout the system. By focusing on culture, Carl Cohn transformed and strengthened an entire system.

CONCLUSION

Sustaining an improvement culture is work that only the superintendent can lead. It is the responsibility of other system leaders, including board and cabinet members, union leaders, and stakeholders to work together toward a collective vision for a community's children. Yet, the superintendent, through words, the design of work, and modelling behavior, sets the tone. Leaders inherit cultures, they must work within a distinct context, and they may feel enormous pressure to make change, all of which can thwart the establishment of a positive improvement culture. And there is no single method for ensuring a culture that engenders equity-based transformation. A leader brings their personal experiences and values to the table, some of which may not jive with those of some schools and members of the community. Yet and still, culture must be the focus of system leaders, because if people aren't working well together to drive an equity agenda, it's likely to fail.

As I found in MCPS, even when there is a track record of success, culture needs to be attended to in order to get to the next level of work. An improvement culture can be sustained through the deliberate actions of system leaders and the design of collaborative work. It can be improved through clear goals and expectations and explicit attention to the language of how educators should work together. Culture is elevated by what a leader says, and more importantly, what they do. An equity-based transformation agenda requires trust among stakeholders. The superintendent is the keeper of that trust and must constantly model it through what they say and what they do.

As Carl Cohn showed, building and elevating an improvement culture that drives an equity agenda is about both knowing your work as a leader and doing more of that, while also modelling what you value and believe. Carl knew that only he could manage the board, so he spent a lot of time doing so, which created the conditions for success. He knew only he could attract the right mix of talent to lead the district, so he went out and found them. He knew that the system needed bold actions to show the new direction, so he took them. Carl also knew that being with people in schools and classrooms would show everyone that what happens in schools is the main thing.

The rule that needs to be rewritten about culture is elegant in its simplicity. There is no policy that can be written, line item placed in the budget, or program to purchase that can attend to culture. An improvement culture that drives an equity lens is sustained by a leader through the actual attention that it gets.

7

Key Leadership Moves

THERE IS NO one way to lead the transformation of a public school system through an equity lens. Every leader brings their own stories and selves to the job. Every community's context is different. The notion of bringing programs to scale, often used as a cudgel by politicians who disparage public schools, is pyrrhic at best. I've been in too many meetings where members of the local funding authority have told me that something that works at one school should just be replicated at another. I resisted these arguments by saying that schools are complex entities and while programs can't be scaled, principles can. Simply taking the same curriculum, professional development, or technology that undergirds one school's successful approach and placing it in another school won't get the same results. It's the same for systems. One leader's redesign of a district may have lessons for other leaders. And certainly, for both schools and districts there are certain universal, evidence-based elements of success that must be adhered to in any transformation. Yet, it is the process of that redesign itself that forms the basis of its eventual effectiveness. How people come together to enact a new, equity-based strategy will spell success or failure.

Leaders can make key moves to engender that success. I think there are six essential ones:

1. Leaders provide political cover.
2. Leaders set clear, nonnegotiable goals.
3. Leaders lead their own learning and that of others.
4. Leaders provide good information and data.

5. Leaders ensure that stakeholders are involved.

6. Leaders engender accountability.

In this chapter, I take these six leadership moves and apply them to the six entry points discussed in previous chapters. I then use the example of Dr. Sonja Brookins Santelises in Baltimore City, Maryland, as an example of a leader who is successfully transforming an urban school system by applying many of the principles of this book.

LEADERS PROVIDE POLITICAL COVER

At its core, the superintendency is a political job. Politics is the effective arbitration of different people's interests, which is what superintendents do all the time. But they must also buffer people within the system and schools from political interference by elected officials and interest groups. The political process sets policy and the budget, yet the same people who make those determinations shouldn't get involved in the daily work of schools. Managing this dynamic can be difficult at best. This principle can be applied to the six entry points of equity-based system transformation in the following ways:

- *Content:* Leaders need to be very clear about why all students need access to standards-based, culturally proficient content. They have to argue publicly and forcefully for the moral imperative of every child having access to high-quality instruction that they can see themselves in.
- *Values:* Leaders need to put their own values on the table. They must be public about why they're doing what they're doing—how it relates to their own story and that of the community—and inspire others to join the journey.
- *Decision-making:* Leaders need to set up processes that take politics into account. If there are contentious interest groups that will thwart a decision, make sure it's accounted for. Elected officials who may support or object to something need to be involved early and often. The actual decision isn't what takes a leader down; rather, it's complaints about the process.

- *Resource allocation:* Leaders must make the tough decision when all else fails. Sometimes the superintendent needs to take the hit and insist on a certain budget cut, reallocation, or the reassignment of a principal. All of the great processes in the world won't completely eliminate the need for a leader to stand on their own and make a call.
- *Talent management:* Leaders need to ensure that the right people are in the right places. This can be a political process, as a school community might view their leader differently than the superintendent. Or stakeholders may not understand why someone was given a central office assignment. People are the number one resource and equity lever that a superintendent has, and political capital may need to be spent to ensure that they're allocated accordingly.
- *Culture:* Leaders need to model espoused behavior. In the political realm, consistency and integrity are essential. One can never expect that everyone will agree with every decision a superintendent makes. And there will be resistance to an equity-based transformation agenda. Stakeholders need to see that the superintendent will fight for what's right in a disciplined and thoughtful way that reflects their collective values.

LEADERS SET CLEAR, NONNEGOTIABLE GOALS

Finding the right balance on the "loose–tight" continuum is one of the greatest leadership challenges for a superintendent. Micromanaging and overprescribing who's going to do what, when, may lead to a quick bump in student learning, but it won't spark the collective effort necessary to achieve lasting gains. Allowing school-level educators too much leeway and decision-making power may result in a lack of coherence, watering down of standards and the perpetuation of inequities. Balance can be found by ensuring there are clear, nonnegotiable goals for both student learning and adult actions. Superintendents must work with the board and community to establish specific expectations for adults to organize around, and then measure progress toward them.

- *Content:* Leaders need to be explicitly clear about what students need to know and be able to do and what adults must do to help them. Benchmarks and milestones should be established regarding what standards all students should achieve by certain key times in their academic careers and how it will eventually lead to college and career readiness.
- *Values:* Leaders must explain why it's important to achieve certain goals. They must be grounded in their own values and those that are shared collectively. It is not enough to just state that all students must achieve a certain standard. Leaders also need to explain why it's important and how it will enable all students to thrive in their futures.
- *Decision-making:* Leaders need to take an interest-based approach to decision-making that centers collective values and equity without overprescribing methods. Process is the essential component here, as how people come together to determine their strategy for achieving a goal will lay the groundwork for its eventual success.
- *Resource allocation:* Leaders must ensure alignment between vision, needs, and resources. New goals can't be achieved without people doing something different every day, which means they need the time to learn. People may need to be reassigned, time may need to be reallocated, and new supporting products or technologies may need to be purchased. Leaders can't expect followers to learn new skills without allocating appropriate resources.
- *Talent management:* Leaders need to have explicit expectations for everyone in the system regarding how and when they will achieve the nonnegotiable goals. Then, they must organize opportunities for people to learn the requisite skills that will enable them to help students achieve.
- *Culture:* Leaders need to focus on the process of how the nonnegotiable goals will be achieved. Culture is built and sustained through people coming together to make decisions. How they do so reflects the culture of the organization. Leaders have to pay close attention to the processes by which stakeholders are engaged in designing, implementing, and adjusting strategies intended to achieve goals.

LEADERS LEAD LEARNING

I've always found it remarkable that educators can be so invested in student learning while disregarding their own and that of others. Superintendents should be accountable for the extent to which they design systems for adults to learn new skills. And they're included in that equation. The best leaders lead their own learning and that of others, and they co-construct that learning while ensuring adherence to relevant and essential content to achieve the district's equity goals.

- *Content:* Leaders need to organize learning around essential skills that educators need in order to serve more students equitably. Such knowledge and skill can be content based or focused on pedagogy, but there must be a straight line between the nonnegotiable goals of the system, the needs of students, the overall vision, and what adults are doing when they're engaged in collective learning.
- *Values:* Leaders must help people understand why they're learning new skills and how it will strengthen the school and larger community. They must also insist that educators are learning about and engaged with others, especially across demographic lines. Educators need to learn about and with people who don't look like them, whether it's students, families, community members, or colleagues.
- *Decision-making:* Leaders need to ensure that all of the necessary information has been gathered to make good decisions and that decisions are aligned to the system's vision and needs. Decision-making is inherently a learning process, as people learn about an issue and each other's interests and values. Leaders can establish explicit processes that build on collective learning about each other's perspectives in order to come out with a better decision.
- *Resource allocation:* Leaders need to ensure that people, time, and funds are explicitly allocated for learning. Whether it's revising the schedule, training teacher leaders, or bringing in outside help, increased student achievement rests on increasing educators' knowledge and skills, which means they have to be learning. Leaders also need to advocate publicly for resources to be allocated to collective learning.

- *Talent management:* Leaders must insist that everyone in the system is in a professional learning community. PLCs are a proven strategy for increasing adults' knowledge and skills. Time and energy must be spent to organize a system-wide strategy to design, implement, assess, and adjust PLCs, as they're effort-intensive. Leaders need to provide the necessary oversight to make that happen.
- *Culture:* Leaders need to model their own learning. There are few things more powerful than a statement from a superintendent that they don't know something but will learn more about it. No one can be expected to know everything about a community or how to best meet new challenges. By modelling learning and engaging in it with others, leaders set a great example.

LEADERS PROVIDE GOOD INFORMATION AND DATA

Superintendents can't manage every aspect of the school system and make every decision, nor should they. They can, however, insist on good processes and comprehensive information for decision-making. Leaders must ask for, and provide, both leading and lagging indicators of how students and adults in the system are performing relative to agreed upon goals. Superintendents must also be transparent and share with the public the information behind their recommendation or decision. Moreover, in the absence of good information, people tend to make up their own stories.

- *Content:* Leaders must be public about leading indicators such as demographic breakdowns of student access and assignment to courses, the cultural relevance of the actual content students are engaged in, and which teachers are assigned to various courses. Formative assessments and student work are great leading indicators of student progress towards standards. Then, they must show the lagging indicators of standards-based summative assessments beyond those mandated by the state.
- *Values:* Leaders must be maximally transparent when sharing information. Assuming it doesn't break any rules, there are few reasons for superintendents not to share information with the public about how the system is doing. This value both instills confidence among stakeholders

and allows for authentic engagement with them to resolve complex issues. Moreover, it's become easier to access information these days, and school districts are rife with rumormongering, so a leader might as well get ahead of the story.

- *Decision-making:* Leaders must establish upfront what information will be used in decision-making processes. Superintendents need to show the public the data that drives the need for a change and what will be used to inform the decision. They should also be clear about the sources in order to mitigate against claims of bias, and multiple ones should be used wherever possible. Since most resistance of equity-based transformation targets the process, leaders have to ensure that the data used to make decisions are comprehensive, accurate, and from multiple perspectives.

- *Resource allocation:* Leaders need to ensure comprehensive data is part of the process of allocating time, talent, and funds. Much like decision-making, resource allocation is all about transparency and having a holistic view of an intended change. Whether it's student and teacher voice, surveys, student performance data, or a landscape analysis, stakeholders deserve to know why resources are being reallocated. After the change, lagging data must be made public to know whether additional adjustments need to be made.

- *Talent management:* Leaders must use information about student and adult performance to to assign talent to task, provide professional learning, and hold people accountable. Superintendents should insist that the best educators serve the most vulnerable students. To do so, they must have a clear standard for educators and then a system for principals and central office staff to act on good information about educators' past performance and effectiveness with different populations in different settings.

- *Culture:* Leaders need to listen to people in order to gather good information. Superintendents need to regularly visit schools and be in multiple parts of the community to understand the hopes, dreams, and needs of students, families, employees, and stakeholders. As leaders go to where people are—rather than having them come to an office—they need to both be transparent and open. By doing so they'll engender trust, which is the essential part of an improvement culture.

LEADERS INSIST ON STAKEHOLDER ENGAGEMENT

Throughout this book I have delineated different ways that leaders can and should involve stakeholders. Internal stakeholders such as students and employees have essential perspectives on the impact and promise of various changes. External stakeholders such as families, community members, and elected officials, have distinct interests that need to be understood and addressed with any transformation effort. All have skin in the game, as public schools serve the community. With every driver of an equity-based transformation effort there's a role for them to play, and superintendents must ensure that both internal and external stakeholders are activated appropriately.

- *Content:* Leaders need to be clear about who gets to decide what gets taught to whom. Since public schools are the ranking and sorting mechanism for American society, an equity agenda requires that superintendents pay close attention to how decisions are made at the local level about access to courses and the content within them. Stakeholder perspective on both can help ensure that the right decisions are made.
- *Values:* Leaders can use the process of developing collective values as a powerful tool to engage disparate groups of stakeholders. Shared values also lay the groundwork for interest-based decision-making, which is essential for transformation agendas. The time spent up front to get the board and key stakeholder groups to agree to a set of values upon which to organize an equity agenda pays off when difficult decisions need to get made.
- *Decision-making:* Leaders must make decisions by including others whenever possible if they want the decision to take hold and last. An equity agenda is strengthened when the voices of the people who are closest to the work, and who are affected by the work, have a say. At the very least, superintendents have an obligation to be transparent by letting stakeholders know how a decision is being made.
- *Resource allocation:* Leaders need to engage with stakeholders to understand both a prospective resource allocation decision and its impact. Whenever possible, stakeholders should be involved

prior to reallocating time, people, or funding as their views can only strengthen the final decision. Superintendents must also gather ongoing feedback about the impact of such decisions.

- *Talent management:* Leaders must tread carefully when engaging stakeholders on issues of talent. Contracts, statutes, and regulations can all complicate decisions about people, and stakeholders may only know one side of a story. Superintendents can, however, use their input to get a holistic view of a particular person's strengths and weaknesses. They can also engage with stakeholders to get a full view of the problem they're trying to solve, which can then make decisions about people appear to be logical and appropriate.

- *Culture:* Leaders need to engage with stakeholders in order to build culture. It's that simple. By visiting schools, engaging with people in their communities, and listening to students, families, and the most disenfranchised, superintendents send clear messages about whose perspectives shape a transformation agenda. The best leaders also let others lead. Improvement cultures are sustained when leadership is distributed throughout the system.

LEADERS ENGENDER ACCOUNTABILITY

My first administrative position was as a director of accountability, so issues of measurement and improvement processes are near and dear to me. Having watched schools and systems change during the NCLB era through Race to the Top and now the Every Student Succeeds Act (ESSA), I have continued to hold two ideas at the forefront of my thinking about how to ensure accountability for equity in school systems. One is the idea I learned from leaders at GE about the "say–do" ratio. If you say you're going to do something, then you better do it. Superintendents need to carefully construct processes by which other leaders make decisions about how they're going to improve, and then they must make sure there's follow through. The other notion is Elmore's reciprocal accountability; I can't hold you accountable for something that you don't know how to do, so it's my responsibility to develop your knowledge and skills to execute our agreed-upon strategy.

- *Content:* Leaders must insist that all content is standards based and they should regularly review and report on which students are taking and succeeding in courses that are aligned to college and career ready standards. Superintendents should put in processes to analyze leading indicators such as student enrollment and course materials, then review lagging indicators such as student achievement. It goes without saying that all of these data must be disaggregated through various metrics.

- *Values:* Leaders need to focus themselves and others on the value of being accountable to each other rather than simply holding people accountable. The latter is relatively easy, as it's based on outcomes and subject to negotiated rules. The former may be more difficult but will lead to sustained improvement. Being accountable to others means that you've internalized the need to work together toward a collective goal and you're part of a community that embraces the need to transform.

- *Decision-making:* Leaders must be accountable to the public—both internal stakeholders and external constituents—by being transparent and following through on what they said they would do. Superintendents will make bad decisions, or they'll make the right decision at the wrong time. It's essential that they take responsibility, explain their reasoning, and then show how they'll make course corrections if necessary.

- *Resource allocation:* Leaders need to ensure that they're investing in building the of capacity of others to fulfill the requirements of an equity agenda. It is not only unfair to expect that people will be able to take on new work without new knowledge and skills, it's a foolhardy stance. Resource allocation is the crux of reciprocal accountability.

- *Talent management:* Leaders must insist that regular and ongoing feedback about the impact of new practices is given and received. To improve, people need to know how they're doing relative to an agreed-upon standard of practice. Superintendents can't supervise every employee, but they can make sure that processes are in place for there to be a continuous improvement cycle that helps people improve through collective learning and clear guidance.

- *Culture:* Leaders need to send positive, factual, and clear messages about what's happening in schools and the system. Superintendents must communicate clearly to various stakeholders about what they're trying to achieve, why it's so important for the community, and how they'll measure their progress. Then, multiple measures must be put in place to track progress toward the standard and stakeholders should be given a number of opportunities to learn about and ask questions.

KINGDOMS RISE AND FALL

Dr. Sonja Brookins Santelises has been the CEO of Baltimore City Public Schools (BCPS) since 2016. She's not new to the city, however, having been the chief academic officer (CAO) under former CEO Andres Alonso from 2007 through 2013. Baltimore is a city with a rich history and tradition of Black excellence that's also had its share of troubles. The school system of nearly 78,000 students, 75 percent of whom are Black, 14 percent Hispanic, and 58 percent low-income, has prepared generations of young people to thrive while neglecting the needs of others. When Sonja was called back by the board and her faith, in the aftermath of the upheaval over Freddie Gray's death at the hands of Baltimore police, she knew that it was her time to step into the top seat.

Sonja fell into teaching serendipitously. She became a founding member of Teach for America (TFA) while substitute teaching and waiting for a placement abroad, as she had been an English and International Relations major in college and was fluent in French. But once she started teaching, Sonja knew that would be her life's work. A series of school leadership roles and consulting led her to graduate school. After settling down with her family she became an assistant and then deputy superintendent in Boston before Andres Alonso enticed her to become Chief Academic Officer (CAO) in Baltimore city. After Andres left, Sonja began to authentically exercise her leadership voice in Washington, DC, working for the Education Trust.

At Education Trust Sonja had the opportunity to aggressively advocate for equity in ways that system leaders simply don't have the luxury of doing. Serving in top leadership in a school system is politically treacherous. Even if you want to call it like it is and speak the truth, there can be consequences. System leaders are always balancing the need to be transparent, data-based, and real about their own values and the needs of the district. But they must also bring people along and gather followers to implement their transformation agenda. Say too little and folks will think you're afraid to address the realities. Say too much and folks will think you're too aggressive and not acknowledging all of their hard work. At Ed Trust, Sonja could write and speak about the urgency of the equity imperative. So when Baltimore City called her back to lead after a few years of turnover in the top seat, Sonja was clear that she was going to do it on her terms.

When Sonja returned, she found that educators were hungry for direction and cohesion in the approach to teaching and learning. While that's her expertise and passion, she also discovered a $130 million budget deficit. Her first eighteen months thus became about organizing a political strategy to get the state to make the district whole. It wasn't easy, and some people doubted her ability to manage finances and operations. But by the end, Sonja had not only rectified the budget situation, she had also gained enormous political capital in the state and back home. Buoyed by her previous success in the district, anchored by her family, as they had been living in the city for eleven years, strengthened with the experience outside of school systems, and armored by her passion for equity and faith, Sonja was ready to drive a teaching and learning agenda.

SPRINKLE THE SEXY

Sonja's approach to transforming BCPS has been slow and steady. While she and others feel incredibly urgent about the need to improve conditions and outcomes for young people, she knows that change takes time. Sonja also arrived at Baltimore at the right time for her kind of leadership. She's a fiercely intelligent and somewhat cerebral leader who's focused on data and what actually works. Baltimore had gone through serious innovation under Alonso, as many urban districts had at that time. But pendulums swing, and the reform community was starting to focus on what Sonja knows how to do as well as anyone else: create a laser-like focus on teaching and learning.

Educators in Baltimore needed direction when Sonja arrived. They wanted coherent curriculum and professional development, some of which her predecessor had started to implement. Yet Sonja also knew that there needed to be symbolic aspects to her transformation agenda. As she said to me, "You have to sprinkle the sexy in a little bit so that people know that change is happening."[1] Having worked in complex urban systems and having studied and supported them, Sonja knew that there was evidence of great practices in other areas. So she used her extensive network to learn how others were doing the work and adopted some of their practices. Whether it was modelling the approach to curriculum reform in DC, or the focus on high school planning in Chicago, Sonja didn't need to be a leader who radically overhauled the system in the name of change. Rather, she has organized a collective and comprehensive effort around a few key core principles of excellence.

Sonja's agenda has been focused on three areas delineated in the BCPS blueprint: student wellness, literacy, staff leadership. The theory of action is clear:

> These areas go hand in hand: If students are motivated and excited about learning, have the skills to think critically, analyze deeply, and express themselves powerfully, and have adults around them who encourage them to persist and excel, they can progress toward high school graduation and postsecondary success.[2]

The blueprint communicates Sonja's values and those of the system. But she has had to change the way the system operates in order to bring it to fruition.

Part of Sonja's focus has been on developing her team. As she said to me, she's not a touchy-feely kind of leader, even though she's incredibly warm in conversation. Knowing that her team needed development to become a cohesive unit, she authorized her special assistant to organize and facilitate her cabinet meetings. (I did the same thing when I was in MCPS, and it was one of the smarter leadership moves I made). Rather than just being a team of really smart people who know how to get results and do whatever they can to make things that they're responsible for happen, they're a true team that works in concert toward the system's goals. They have focused meetings and regular retreats where they address both the ongoing administrative items of the system and the big-picture work they want to do. They've tackled issues of race and equity in deep ways in order to ensure they practice what they preach. And they sustain each other's work through a focus on what matters most for an equity agenda.

Sonja knows that systems transformation rests on a clear vision for teaching and learning, supports for educators to learn new skills, and the activation and engagement of community. She has a comprehensive approach to adopting new curriculum, with an express eye toward cultural competency. She had to activate student voice to convince all parts of the community that such an approach was needed. But she also makes sure to give educators a lot of time to work through new curriculum and make it their own. Sonja and her team use comprehensive data to drive their decisions and are brutally honest with each other, the board, and the public about the realities of the challenges and needs. She's clear that there's a lot of work to be done and that she won't be the one to finish the job. But she's laying a strong foundation with her deliberate approach.

Sonja has also had to "listen to the street" as she's been transforming the system. She sees her work as a calling to create a generational shift for young people and families. Baltimore will be made stronger through a steady focus on rebuilding public systems that support children and families, and schools are the cornerstone. But she's had to get back out into the community to engage with leaders, community member, families, educators, and students to show that she's both listening to them and will lead them where they need to go.

Like other leaders profiled in this book, Sonja is driven and grounded by her faith and makes no bones about it. All leaders need a core if they're going to do this work. They need to not be so afraid of losing the job that they'll do anything to keep it. Sonja's strength comes from her deep faith, which gives her a sense of peace and calm as she goes about the work of transformation. She's constantly communicating her strategy and approach to multiple audiences and does so in a calm and steady way that sometimes masks her sense of urgency and passion. That's what thoughtful, capable, intelligent leaders do.

CONCLUSION

The context and culture of Baltimore may be unique, but the leadership moves that Sonja has had to make to drive an equity-based transformation strategy are similar to those of others in the superintendency. There is no one-size-fits-all approach, even though there are clear nonnegotiable elements of improvement and equity. Superintendents have to be thoughtful and deliberate about how they're going to engage in collective transformation efforts. They must be intentional about understanding all aspects of their systems, communicating the realities to stakeholders, ensuring they have the right team in place to enact change, and processes that will activate internal and external partners to make it all happen. There's no single approach to tying it all together on behalf of children, just like there's no single blueprint to build a house, even if all of the elements are familiar.

Great systems leadership is about having a big-picture vision for what's possible when adults do their absolute best on behalf of young people. It's also about knowing which levers to pull and when. Perhaps most importantly, it's about knowing the right questions to ask. If the answers were clear, we wouldn't have so many challenges in our public school systems that serve vulnerable students. Yes, there are core strategies and similar practices in schools and districts that serve all children well. But the paradox of leadership lies in knowing that a successful approach in one context may not work in another. Leaders who deeply understand this, and know who they are at their core, will be able to embrace the complexity.

CONCLUSION

We Make the Road by Walking

I've often told leaders and politicians that it's possible to scale principles, but not programs. Some stakeholders believe that if a certain approach works in one setting, then it should be imported into another. The elusive search for replicability may serve the interests of the marketplace or be attractive to elected officials, but the realities of school systems don't allow for such simplicity. I wish it were otherwise. It would be wonderful if leaders in one district could just plug in the algorithm that worked in another district and get similar results. As I've tried to convey in this book, there is no curriculum, technology, professional development, or program one can buy that, on its own, will lead to better results. The key to systems transformation is how a system leader uses those tools through an equity lens and a social justice stance to organize people to act in different ways in support of the most vulnerable students. Yes, what adults do is important. There are clearly known successful practice that lead to improved student learning. We know what great teaching and leadership look like. But to improve the practice of every educator in a system is no easy feat. To shift the distribution of average takes a thoughtful and systematic approach.

My leadership journey started in Brooklyn but was cemented in Cambridge, Massachusetts, in the Harvard Graduate School of Education (HGSE) Urban Superintendents Program (USP). It was there that my small cohort of doctoral students learned theory and practice. At HGSE we were surrounded by the best academics who knew the evidence about what works to improve schools and systems. In addition, the USP leaders, Linda Wing and Bob Peterkin, made sure to build a network of practitioners who were actually doing the work in school systems to help us turn theory into practice. It was there that I learned what it takes to transform a school system through an equity lens.

Back in 1998, when I started at Harvard, equity was not on everyone's minds. Sure, the standards movement had begun, and we were discovering the stark realities of achievement of different groups of students within and among school districts. But unlike today, equity wasn't at the forefront of most school system leaders' minds. It wasn't until NCLB came down a few years later and superintendents were forced to face reality that we began to hear more about how to organize an equity agenda. I felt like my USP peers and I were ahead of the game.

When I set out to write this book, I knew that I would revisit the stories that I knew from many of my fellow USPers. Everyone who's been through that program has a bond. Even if we don't know each other well personally, we know that a USPer has a titanium core focused on equity and excellence in teaching and learning. Bob and Linda didn't let you in the program—or allow you to stay—if you didn't have that commitment. As I sought to tell stories about leaders who have tried to transform their systems, who have rewritten the rules, and who embrace the complexity, I knew I'd go with who I know.

Not all the leaders in this book have come from the USP network. Some I've gotten to know from my work at PDK. But all of them have shown the ability to organize an equity agenda in a thoughtful and deliberate way. As I listened to these leaders tell their stories and then tried to convey the lessons in these pages, a few themes emerged. In the following, I briefly recap some of those key themes and tenets, and then suggest how they can lead to a new approach to accountability system design and what they imply for leadership.

DON'T SLASH AND BURN

It's clear to me that "slash and burn" leadership doesn't lead to actual transformation. Great system leaders find the right balance between the urgency of the moral imperative and their embrace of the complexity of actually doing the job. It would be wonderful if the promises of radically overhauling a district led to long-standing change. Don't get me wrong; there are some aspects of school systems that should be done away with and some innovations that need be put in place. Moreover, our kids can't wait. But great superintendents understand that the work of transforming a school system is fundamentally about getting adults to adopt new practices. Adults don't learn new knowledge and skills quickly, and there are good reasons why they shouldn't. The promises that a new technology, curriculum, program, structure, or policy will lead to quick and large gains in student learning simply don't ring true for the leaders that I profiled in this book. They do, however, organize their efforts around a few core tenets of transformation, all of which can be found in the literature.

All of them speak to the need to have good data upon which to make decisions and to share that information and their system's reality transparently with stakeholders. Data alone doesn't drive improvement. Simply stating a fact won't spur people to change. Data does, however, anchor stories of need and aspiration. One of my mantras is that at best, data help you ask better questions. Great system leaders start with the data, then organize processes for stakeholders to probe into it and see where it leads. They "drill down." Whether that's further analysis of existing data or the collection of complementary qualitative data such as student voice, effective system leaders use data to begin unravelling the real issues facing their district.

Every chapter in this book seemed to come back to the primacy of the principal. To my mind, the principal is the most important position in the system. Hence, the selection, development, support, and supervision of principals is the most important job of system leaders. Principals must be supported to be leaders of their own learning, while also engaging and developing their own communities as they embrace a new equity agenda. Superintendents must ensure that the work of central office doesn't interfere with a principal's ability to drive improvement, while also building a degree of cohesiveness among disparate schools. It's a delicate balance to strike, but the most effective system leaders keep their eyes on how they can support the work of principals and make sure that everyone around them is doing the same.

Part of a superintendent's work in supporting principals' improvement efforts is establishing their own high-functioning team to move the work through. While I didn't pay explicit attention to this issue throughout this book, I know from my experience and that of others that a superintendent's cabinet is a key lever to pull in order to make the work actually happen. Creating such a team is hard, though. New superintendents have to determine whether the people already in those positions should stay. Many of them have long-standing relationships with principals, elected officials and board members, and stakeholders. Superintendents who come through the ranks may find themselves supervising former colleagues or bucking tradition and culture by bringing in new people. Yet the work of transformation doesn't happen without the right people organizing others to get the work done. Whether it's new approaches to managing talent or allocating resources, or the ongoing work of principal supervision, a superintendent's cabinet can make or break an equity agenda. Successful transformation rests on solid processes to organize adult work. Cabinet members create and oversee those processes.

Effective system leaders are intentional in their inquiry and discovery processes. This work should begin before even starting the job through a comprehensive transition process that objectively identifies strengths and weaknesses and begins to create a shared story. A superintendent's entry, where they get to know the community's values and they make their own story public, helps to build trust and the foundation for collective effort. Regular visits to schools are manifestations of a leader's values and show stakeholders that they value the work of educators above all else. They also help build an understanding of a school's culture and readiness to embrace an equity agenda. Great leaders ask open-ended questions and are active listeners who learn the interests of various stakeholder groups so that they can make collective decisions. This all takes time and, again, doesn't lend itself to quick fixes. But the investment in discovery lays the groundwork for transformation.

It goes without saying that the most effective system leaders are also the best communicators. They are authentic in sharing their own story, values, and vision. Great leaders also use multiple mediums to communicate with a broad set of stakeholders. Whether it's small groups, one-on-one, the written word, or social or traditional media, superintendents who successfully lead an equity agenda communicate "seven times, seven ways," as Larry Leverett always said. They use the data to frame the need, organize engagement processes for collective effort to address challenges and meet aspirations, and celebrate progress and achievements while being transparent about the ongoing work of the system.

I hesitate to name political acuity as a discrete tenet of successful system leadership, because everything superintendents do is about the effective arbitration of different people's interests. But what has become clear to me in writing this book is the need for a sophisticated approach to knowing when to push or pull and when to hold or fold. The "big P" politics of navigating elected officials so that they'll support a new policy or budget certainly consumes the public's attention, as does a crisis or controversial decision. But the daily interactions among people that get them to change their minds about an issue or accept a new approach are where the rubber hits the road. The "small p" politics of constantly having an ear to the ground and developing a gut sense of whether something will fly or fail is equally important to an equity-based transformation effort.

Finally, one of the major themes that emerged while writing this book is that the most effective leaders know themselves. The superintendency is hard. I loved it and took great pride and joy in my work. But there's no doubt that it can be brutal job. Leaders need to know why they're doing it and what grounds them. They need to be able to walk away and can never be afraid to get fired for doing what they know to be right. Great leaders are grounded, whether it be in their faith, their conviction, or their beliefs about what's possible for young people and communities. It's impossible to be an effective systems leader without knowing why you do what you do and what will make you happy. If you need a "kid fix," then visit schools regularly. If you love articulating your vision, then create opportunities to write and speak. If you feed off the energy of stakeholder engagement, then get deeply involved in working with different communities. Whatever it may be, its essential that system leaders know what makes them tick and then do more of that.

WHAT'S NEXT FOR SCHOOL SYSTEMS

Writing this book has given me a lot of time to think about what I would do if I ever find myself leading another school system. And I seem to always return to my roots as an accountability guy. When I started designing accountability systems in the late 1990s, it was somewhat of a blank slate. Pre-NCLB, we didn't have major federal and state laws to guide school improvement efforts. We could use the research, stakeholder engagement, and collective effort to drive an equity agenda. Now that we've entered a new era of ESSA, with the COVID-19 pandemic barely in our rearview mirrors, there's an opportunity to build on what we've learned about good accountability practices.

To my mind there are four "buckets" of data that superintendents and communities should be looking at to drive a transformational equity agenda: adult, student, family, and environmental. Granted, none of these are surprising, innovative, or new to those who have been leading the work for a while. But how they're pulled together in a coherent framework that identifies needs and vision is the true test.

By adult data, I mean the knowledge and information we have about the people in the system. I've said over and over in this book that people not only make up the bulk of a district's budget, they're also the number one equity lever. But what do we know about their effectiveness, and how is that knowledge used when making decisions? So much of our focus is on student-level data, especially their performance on state standardized tests and commensurate measures of academic progress. This is little surprise, given both the public nature of accountability systems and the ready availability of student performance data. Yet, if systems improvement is all about adult learning, what do we know about whether adults have the requisite knowledge and skills to drive an equity agenda? When looking at a group of students' achievements, does the principal know how similar students did in the same teacher's class in previous years? Are there patterns in the data that might help the principal understand whether a particular teacher has a distinct strength or need in a content area?

Adults also work within a distinct context and enter into their work with previous experiences. Their performance should be understood as part of a series that has led them to their current position and is influenced by their surroundings. Since most teachers attend institutes of higher education from within their state, system leaders should know which programs tend to produce more effective educators. They must understand the developmental needs of new staff. Recruiting and hiring processes can help determine strengths and needs, and when done right, supervision and evaluation can be a source of useful information to help educators improve. Perceptual data about schools should also be gathered, as it helps principal supervisors understand the culture of a school and levels of engagement, both of which are essential elements of an equity agenda. Special attention has to be paid to the conditions under which educators of color work, as they tend to leave more readily if not supported. Superintendents have the obligation to gather such data about adults to better understand how they'll organize systems to improve adult practice.

Information about students drives nearly every improvement effort in schools and districts. This is no surprise, given the public and political nature of education, and that the student is the effect of our treatment. Student achievement is the ultimate outcome of schools, so measuring it is essential to knowing whether adult actions are having the desired impact. There is no avoiding state standardized tests and other academic measures, nor should there be, whether we like it or not. Measures of progress are important to know whether students are more likely to achieve standards. Metrics such as graduating college and career readiness should also be milestones to organize around. Lately, measures of SEL and engagement have taken hold of the collective imagination of school and system leaders. All of these can be brought together and analyzed to help system leaders understand patterns and develop interventions to help all students be on the path to graduating on time.

Early warning indicator systems are built on algorithms that combine multiple sets of data about students in order to predict whether or not a student is more likely than not to graduate on time and ready. There are different metrics that can be input into such systems, including course grades, behavior, and attendance. These leading indicators of performance can predict lagging indicators such as achievement on standardized tests and graduation. On their own, however, they do little good. System leaders must use such data to spur action and interventions at the school and community level. It should be used to "name names" by not making assumptions about a student but by starting an inquiry cycle to understand underlying causes. A student may be acting out because of a problem at home, or because they're being bullied. They may be missing school because they need to tend to a relative or they had to move out of their rental apartment again. Their lack of achievement may be related to a distinct instructional strategy that their teacher is, or is not, using. We have processes to deal with that. But the student's real story must be known by adults so that they and their families can get the services and supports they need from within the school and the community.

System leaders should allocate resources to schools so that they can not only understand each child's story but also that of their family and community. Such information can be sensitive and requires highly trained people who know how to interact with and support adults, especially if they're from different demographic backgrounds. Yet it's essential, as family dynamics can play as much of a role in student achievement as schools. There are a few different ways to look at information about families and community. Certainly, marital and employment status can help paint a picture, given their association with student achievement. Other contextual information may be about income, housing status, availability of wi-fi, and other relatives living in the house. If possible, any knowledge about family health can inform a school's understanding of the challenges a student may face. These data can be hard to collect and should never be collected impersonally. Schools need to build trust with families to get a full picture of their stories so that they can provide proper supports.

System leaders should also help schools understand the larger environment that children are in. Food and housing insecurity are major drivers of low achievement and readiness for school. The availability of public transportation can help or hinder parents' ability to be gainfully employed. Social services can play a supporting role in a family's success, and access to them can be determined by asset mapping and landscape analysis. System leaders should be gathering and organizing these kinds of data in accessible displays so that school leaders understand the needs, conditions, and resources available to their students.

When data from these different domains are brought together it can give system leaders and decision-makers more insight into some of the real issues facing their students and communities. All actions happen within a context. An educator's effectiveness happens within the school they work in and the degree to which it supports their ongoing learning and improvement. A child's performance and learning happen within the school, their family, and their community. A comprehensive picture of all of these factors can help a superintendent allocate resources and make decisions that are aligned to actual needs and strengths and not dependent on the narrow metric of state standardized tests.

THE EQUITY IMPERATIVE

Throughout this book I've tried to describe the equity issues leaders face when trying to transform a school system. Some core equity practices are clearly evident in their approaches and the literature. I believe that system leaders who are trying to drive an equity agenda need to have a few stakes in the ground to organize their efforts around. Below I briefly delineate what I think those are.

The first stake in the ground is standards for both students and adults. Leaders need to have a vision for excellence in achievement and practice. They must describe that vision and tell stories about it. Standards give clarity to everyone about what schools are trying to achieve and how they will get there. State academic standards are an unavoidable part of this equation, but they're a starting point. Standards from a professional association, such as NCTM or the National Council of Teachers of English (NCTE), industry certification aligned to a CTE program, acceptance at the state university without remediation, or attainment of college credit while in high school, are all north stars that can be used to determine benchmarks for students to achieve throughout their schooling. We also know what great adult practice looks like. National Board certification can serve as an external guidepost for adults to achieve. Evaluation systems should describe distinct practices that educators should evidence as they engage with young people and adults. Standards for achievement and practice allow for system-wide cohesion. They also force the question of whether all students in every school have opportunities to attain them.

The second stake in the ground for system leaders to organize around is whether all students have access to high-quality instruction that will enable them to attain the system's standards. Access is the starting point for equity. Public education is the ranking and sorting mechanism for American society, and too many diverse school systems formally and informally segregate students of different demographic groups through entry exams, placement tests, and course assignment policies. White parents, in particular, use these mechanisms to justify their continued participation in, and support for, their local public school system. Elected officials and many system and school leaders are wary of the politics of doing away with them while also not knowing what else to do and how to change. Yet, simply put, all students having access to high-quality, standards-based instruction is the true measure of a system leader's commitment to an equity agenda.

Equity agendas are strengthened through stakeholder engagement, the third stake in the ground. Moreover, stakeholders have the right to know why a systems transformation is happening and what it will mean for their children, their work, and their community. While it's tempting to make radical changes in the face of clear moral imperatives, superintendents who fail to engage stakeholders run a big risk of being ousted for lack of public support. Let me be clear, the act of community engagement alone will not win everyone over and get them to accept an equity agenda. But, engaging with politically powerful groups and individuals is necessary, as it's expected of a superintendent, and by not doing so a leader puts a big target on their backs. Leaders can also model their values by engaging stakeholders who aren't the "usual suspects." They can go out into the community to engage with traditionally disenfranchised families and communities. They can spend a lot of time with teachers and support professionals, in addition to time spent with principals. They can talk with students and get their perspectives on the work. All of these stakeholders can be activated as supporters and leaders, and their efforts can make a transformation that much better.

Collective effort is another essential part of an equity-based approach to systems transformation. Formal and informal groups must be seen as additive energy and power to a system leader's efforts. I know full well that some of these groups may do everything they can to thwart an equity agenda. Employee associations, board members, elected officials, and politically powerful constituent groups may all actively work against equity, or at least the leader's process for enacting their agenda. Leaders have to achieve a delicate balance of aggressively pushing for necessary change while making sure that people who want to be part of the solution and have something to contribute can join. Deliberate and intentional processes based on shared interests can help bring people into a collective transformation effort.

System leaders who are driving an equity agenda must also surround themselves with the right people. Superintendents do little of the actual work that happens in school systems. Their cabinets, central office leaders, principals, and informal advisors are all key ingredients to driving transformation. Leaders have to manage the tension between insiders and outsiders and don't want to bring in all new people at once. And there may be great untapped talent within the system that's just waiting for a chance to lead. But no leader goes it alone. They must receive real feedback on their own practice, insight from others who know what's happening on the ground, expertise from leaders steeped in content and practice, and unconditional loyalty and support when facing the public. Without having the right leaders around them, a superintendent doesn't stand a chance.

With the right team and an engaged community, superintendents can make strategic resource allocation moves, another stake in the ground. The distribution of time, talent, and funds will enable an equity agenda to thrive or stall. Transformation will not happen just because someone named the need for it. Adults must change their daily practices with young people and each other. To do so they need time to learn new skills, and leaders must provide the commensurate guidance and support. Students who are not yet at standard need to accelerate their progress. This requires that they have the most effective teachers and the time to improve their knowledge and skills. None of this will happen without a deliberate, strategic, and transparent approach to allocating resources. Moreover, the allocation of resources allows for reciprocal accountability, as no one can be expected to do something new without first learning how to do so. A leader can't hold someone accountable if they haven't provided the necessary supports.

Over and over in this book I've come back to the principle of adult learning. No matter who it is, everyone in a system needs to actively and collectively learn. Equity agendas and system transformation are hard and complex. If they weren't, everyone would enact them, and our schools would be in better shape. Both the technical and adaptive leadership skills needed to drive an equity agenda must be learned. There's tension here, as there's a moral imperative to act quickly and boldly in the face of inequities. Moreover, the public, elected officials, and the media often have no patience for an incremental approach. Yet learning takes time. There's no right answer to alleviating this tension, but leaders have to understand it and find opportunities to act boldly while also organizing systems for adults to learn new practices.

Finally, and perhaps most importantly, the transformation of public school systems through an equity lens requires that leaders are culturally proficient. I haven't explicitly attended to this stake-in-the-ground in this book, as many others have done so much better than I ever will. I also assume that a leader who is likely to read this book has already started their own journey and doesn't need me to reinforce what we already know about the need for white people, in particular, to learn how to engage authentically with individuals and communities of color. It is, however, a necessary component of any equity agenda. Cultural proficiency must be evidenced in how talent is recruited, hired, supported, managed, and distributed. It needs to be an underpinning of curriculum and materials decisions. As white leaders engage with different groups of young people, families, and community members, they must learn how to center stories different then their own. I could go on, and again, many others have. What's nonnegotiable to an equity-based transformation agenda is that everyone, especially the superintendent, has embraced their journey to cultural proficiency.

LET MY PEOPLE GO

In writing this book I've continually returned in my mind to two realities of school district leadership. The first is that no matter how hard you work, how much you accomplish, and how different a system looks many years into your tenure, the work is never done. I ask leaders all the time whether they are Moses or Joshua. Faith doesn't play a big role in my life, but I like the metaphor because it suggests that some people need to break stuff up and others need to put them back together. It's possible for some leaders to do both, although it's highly unusual. The best a leader can hope for is to start or build on a transformation effort. You may be the one to break the shackles that bind a system to old ways of thinking. You may need to ensure that old practices are eradicated before the new work begins. Or you may be the one to lead a new generation of educators as they embrace the hard work of equity and create a better place. Knowing which role you play is a key to success.

Another useful metaphor is that of building a house. A superintendent can put a foundation in place for the next generation of leaders; they may even be able to draw the blueprints and start construction. Or they may be the one to come in and do renovations or even tear it down and start anew. But it's hard to lead every phase of design, construction, and outfitting, and then be the one to do the renovations a few years later. New leaders bring different perspectives and must be developed and discovered so that they can bring their insights and energy to new challenges. And the superintendency is hard work. It requires physical, mental, and spiritual energy to meet its challenges for fifteen hours a day, every single day. The best leaders know when they can no longer give everything that the job demands.

The second reality that kept emerging as I wrote this book is that leaders need to be honest about what's possible. People in a system can only learn so much and do so much at once. The urgency that superintendents feel when they're trying to drive an equity agenda will not be shared by everyone. Moreover, rewriting rules is difficult work. There are technical, statutory, political, and cultural issues to face. There are few clear right answers, only different choices and possibilities. It's really hard to take a deep breath and say, no, we're going to have to wait to do something, even when you know that not doing so will maintain a status quo that's not serving vulnerable children. In fact, it's the hardest part of being a superintendent. Seeing a clear injustice or problem that needs to be fixed and not being able to do so immediately can be painful. But the alternative can be worse. I've seen situations where the house is designed, the foundation is poured, the frame is built, and then the house just sits there for years because the mortgage didn't come through. Leaders who start something and don't set it up to be finished can do harm to a system because of the wasted energy that needs to be recovered and rebuilt for the next leader.

Systems transformation through an equity lens is incredibly complex work. My own experience and that of the leaders I've profiled in this book can hopefully bring some insight to the work of superintendents and system leaders who are climbing new hills. Just as I always say about data—at best, it helps you ask questions—superintendents need to constantly have an inquiry stance. Few situations a system leader face are crystal clear, and no decisions a superintendent makes are cut and dry. Rather, leaders need to surround themselves with the right people who will help them probe, ask questions, and develop and implement new solutions to age-old problems. Rewriting the rules isn't always about finding the newest, brightest, shiniest object. It's about pulling apart the layers that have calcified for generations and left too many children languishing in our public schools. Thankfully, we have enough evidence of what can work to transform systems that it shouldn't take another generation before those layers are transformed into something that will better serve each and every one of our students, in every classroom, every day.

Notes

Introduction

1. Meredith I. Honig and Lydia R. Rainey, *How Districts Can Support Deeper Learning: The Need for Performance Alignment* (Boston: Jobs For the Future, 2015).
2. D. Goldhaber, V. Quince, & R. Theobald, "Teacher Quality Gaps in U.S. Public Schools: Trends, Sources, and Implications." *Phi Delta Kappan*, 100, no. 8 (2019): 14–19.
3. Ray Callahan, *Education and the Cult of Efficiency* (Chicago: University of Chicago Press, 1962).
4. Jal Mehta, *The Allure of Order* (New York: Oxford University Press, 2013).
5. Karl E. Weick, "Educational Organizations as Loosely Coupled Systems," *Administrative Science Quarterly*, 21, no. 1 (March 1976): 1–19.
6. Richard F. Elmore, "Building a New Structure for School Leadership," *American Educator* (Winter 1999–2000).
7. Mehta, *The Allure of Order*, 40.
8. Donald J. Peurach et al., "From Mass Schooling to Education Systems: Changing Patterns in the Organization and Management of Instruction," *Review of Research in Education*, 43 (March 2019): 32–67.
9. Peurach et al., "From Mass Schooling to Education Systems," 43.
10. Thomas S. Dee et al., "The Impact of No Child Left Behind on Students, Teachers, and Schools [with Comments and Discussion]," *Brookings Papers on Economic Activity* (2010): 149–207.
11. Peurach et al., "From Mass Schooling to Education Systems," 47.
12. Honig and Rainey, *How Districts Can Support Deeper Learning*.

Chapter 1

1. College Board, 10th *Annual AP Report to the Nation* (New York, 2014).
2. Connecticut Advisory Committee to the Commission on Civil Rights, *School Desegregation in Stamford, CT, A Report* (1977).
3. "Stamford Board of Education Policies," https://www.stamfordpublicschools.org/sites/g/files/vyhlif3841/f/uploads/6000_policies_4.pdf
4. Brian Osborne (former superintendent, South Orange Maplewood, NJ), in discussion with the author, June 2020.

5. "De-Leveling the System: A Community Speaks," Crizlassic Productions (2012, https://www.youtube.com/watch?v=SnhWRtMqORM

6. John A. Dossey, Sharon Soucy McCrone, and Katherine Taylor Halvorsen, *Mathematics Education in the United States, 2016*. Thirteenth International Congress on Mathematics Education (Hamburg, 2016).

7. IES: National Center for Educational Statistics, *"Average National Assessment of Educational Progress (NAEP) Mathematics Scale Score and Percentage of Students Attaining NAEP Mathematics Achievement Levels, by Selected School and Student Characteristics and Grade: Selected Years, 1990 Through 2019,"* https://nces.ed.gov/programs/digest/d19/tables/dt19_222.12.asp

8. Robert Q. Berry III and Matthew R. Larson, "How to Catalyze Change in High School Mathematics," *Phi Delta Kappan*, 100, no. 6 (February 2019): 39–44.

9. Richard F. Elmore, "Building a New Structure for School Leadership," *American Educator* (Winter 1999–2000).

Chapter 2

1. Kenneth Leithwood, *Strong Districts and Their Leadership*, Institute for Educational Leadership (Ontario, 2013).

2. Rosabeth Moss Kanter, *Supercorp* (New York: Crown Business, 2009).

3. Larry Leverett (former superintendent, Plainfield, NJ), in discussion with the author, September, 2020.

4. Larry Leverett

5. Larry Leverett

6. John P. Kotter, "Accelerate!," *Harvard Business Review* (November, 2012).

7. Marshall Ganz, "Public Narrative, Collective Action, and Power." In *Accountability Through Public Opinion: From Inertia to Public Action*, eds. Sina Odugbemi and Taeku Lee (Washington, DC: The World Bank, 2011): 273–289.

8. Barry Jentz, with Joan Wofford, *Entry: The Hiring, Start-Up & Supervision of Administrators* (New York: McGraw-Hill: 1982).

9. William Bridges, *Managing Transitions: Making the Most of Change* (Philadelphia: Da Capo Press, 2009).

10. Beth Schiavino Narvaez (former superintendent, Hartford, CT), in discussion with the author, September 2020.

Chapter 3

1. Christopher H. Tienken, ed., *The American Superintendent 2020 Decennial Study* (London: Rowman & Littlefield, 2021).

2. John Carver, *Boards that Make a Difference* (San Francisco: Jossey-Bass, 2006).

3. Meredith I. Honig and Lydia R. Rainey, *Supervising Principals for Instructional Leadership: A Teaching and Learning Approach* (Cambridge, MA: Harvard Education Press, 2020).

4. Jack Schneider and Andrew Saultz, "Authority and Control, the Tension at the Heart of Standards-Based Accountability," *Harvard Education Review*, 90, no. 3 (Fall 2020).

5. Roger Fisher and William Ury, *Getting to Yes: Negotiating Agreement Without Giving In* (New York: Penguin, 1991).

6. Margaret Wheatley, *Leadership and the New Science* (San Francisco: Berrett-Koehler, 1992).

Chapter 4

1. Rebecca A. Thessin and Joshua P. Starr, "Supporting the Growth of Effective Professional Learning Communities," *Phi Delta Kappan*, 42, no. 6 (March 2011).
2. Learning First, *Integrating Quality Professional Development into the Daily Lives of Teachers: Insights from High-Performing Systems* (2014).
3. Thessin and Starr, "Supporting the Growth of Effective Professional Learning Communities."
4. Tim Hodges, "School Engagement Is More Than Just Talk," Gallup, October 25, 2018, https://www.gallup.com/education/244022/school-engagement-talk.aspx.
5. Lori Nazareno, "4 Steps for Redesigning Time for Student and Teacher Learning," *Phi Delta Kappan*, 98, no. 4 (December 2016/January 2017).
6. Nathan Levenson, *Six Shifts to Improve Special Education and Other Interventions: A Common Sense Approach for School Leaders* (Cambridge: Harvard Education Press, 2020).
7. Levenson, *Six Shifts.*
8. Sun Tzu, *The Art of War*, trans. Thomas Cleary (Boston: Shambhala Publications, 1988).
9. Deinya Phenix et al., "A Forced March for Failing Schools: Lessons from the New York City Chancellor's District," *Education Policy Analysis Archives* 13, no. 40 (September 28, 2005).
10. Deinya Phenix et al., "A Forced March for Failing Schools: Lessons from the New York City Chancellor's District," *Education Policy Analysis Archives* 13, no. 40 (September 28, 2005).

Chapter 5

1. Daniel Weisberg, et al., *The Widget Effect: Our National Failure to Acknowledge and Act on Differences in Teacher Effectiveness* (The New Teacher Project, 2006).
2. James C. Collins, *Good to Great: Why Some Companies Make the Leap . . . and Others Don't* (New York: Harper Collins, 2001).
3. Linda Darling Hammond, "Teacher Quality and Student Achievement: A Review of State Policy Evidence," *Education Policy Analysis Archives*, 8, no. 1 (January, 2000).
4. David D. Leibowitz and Lorna Porter, "The Effect of Principal Behaviors on Student, Teacher, and School Outcomes: A Systematic Review and Meta-Analysis of the Empirical Literature," *Review of Educational Research*, 89, no. 5 (October 2019): 785–827.
5. Linda Darling Hammond, "Inequality in Teaching and Schooling: How Opportunity Is Rationed to Students of Color in America," *National Academy of Sciences* (2001), https://www.ncbi.nlm.nih.gov/books/NBK223640/
6. Desiree Carver-Thomas, "Diversifying the Teaching Profession: How to Recruit and Retain Teachers of Color," Palo Alto California, Learning Policy Institute, (2018).
7. Dan Goldhaber, Roddy Theobald, and Christopher Tien, "Why we need a diverse teacher workforce," *Phi Delta Kappan*, 100, no. 5 (2019): 25–30.
8. US Department of Education, Office of Planning, Evaluation and Policy Development, Policy and Program Studies Service, *The State of Racial Diversity in the Educator Workforce* (Washington, DC, 2016).
9. US Department of Education, *The State of Racial Diversity.*
10. Jessica Yin and Lisette Partelow, *An Overview of the Alternative Teacher Certification Sector Outside of Higher Education* (Washington, DC: Center for American Progress, 2020).
11. Lisette Partelow, *What to Make of Declining Enrollment in Teacher Preparation Programs* (Washington, DC: Center for American Progress, 2019).
12. Ed O'Boyle, "4 Things Gen Z and Millennials Expect from Their Workplace," Gallup (March 30, 2021), https://www.gallup.com/workplace/336275/things-gen-millennials-expect-workplace.aspx

13. Carver-Thomas, *Diversifying the Teaching Profession*.
14. Ben Jensen et al., "Beyond PD: Teacher Professional Learning in High-Performing Systems" (Washington, DC: National Center on Education and the Economy, 2016).
15. Jal Mehta, *The Allure of Order: High Hopes, Dashed Expectations, and the Troubled Quest to Remake American Schooling* (New York: Oxford University Press, 2015).
16. Gallup, https://news.gallup.com/poll/1597/confidence-institutions.aspx
17. Gallup, *Employee Engagement and Performance: Latest Insights from the World's Largest Study* (Washington, DC: Gallup, 2020).
18. Carver-Thomas, *Diversifying the Teaching Profession*.
19. Richard F. Elmore, "Building a New Structure for School Leadership," *American Educator* (Winter 1999–2000).

Chapter 6

1. Susan Moore Johnson *Where Teachers Thrive* (Cambridge: Harvard Education Press, 2019); Matthew A Kraft and John P. Papay, "Can Professional Environments in Schools Promote Teacher Development? Explaining Heterogeneity in Returns to Teaching Experience." *Educational Effectiveness and Policy Analysis [Internet]*, 36, no. 4 (2014): 476–500; Esther Quintero, Ed., *Teaching in Context: The Social Side of Education Reform* (Cambridge: Harvard Education Press, 2017). Penny Bender Sebring, et al., *The Essential Supports for School Improvement*, (Consortium on School Research at the University of Chicago, 2006). Richard M. Ingersoll, Philip Sirinides, and Patrick Dougherty, "Leadership Matters, Teachers Role in School Decision Making and School Performance," *American Educator* (Spring 2018): 13–17.
2. Lee G. Bolman and Terrence E. Deal, *Reframing Organizations: Artistry, Choice, and Leadership* (San Francisco: Jossey-Bass, 1997), p. 214.
3. Mark A. Smylie, "Three Organizational Lessons for School Improvement," *Thinking and Actins Systemically, Improving School Districts Under Pressure*, edited by Alan J. Daly and Kara S. Finnigan (AERA, 2016).
4. Alan J. Daly, Kara S. Finnigan, and Yi-Hwa Liou, "The Social Cost of Leadership Churn: The Case of an Urban School District," Ed. Esther Quintero, *Teaching in Context: The Social Side of School Reform* (Cambridge: Harvard Education Press), p. 133.
5. Montgomery County Public Schools, "Strategic Planning Framework: Building Our Future Together," 2012.
6. MCPS framework.
7. National School Reform Faculty, Harmony Education Center, https://nsrfharmony.org/

Chapter 7

1. Sonja Santelises (CEO, Baltimore City Public Schools), in discussion with the author, June 28, 2021.
2. Baltimore City Public Schools, "Blueprint for Success," https://www.baltimorecityschools.org/blueprint

Acknowledgments

About four years ago, I was hiking with my family and I mentioned to my youngest son (who was eight or nine at the time) that I was thinking about writing a book. When his eyes opened wide and he responded with amazement that his dad could actually do such a thing, I knew I had to follow through. This book rests on the shoulders of all of the people I've come to know during my quarter-century as a public educator. My son's wonderment has held me accountable as the lessons I've learned from mentors, colleagues, and friends has filled the pages.

Bob Peterkin and Linda Wing, former co-directors of the Harvard University Graduate School of Education Urban Superintendents Program, plucked me from obscurity in Brooklyn, New York, and put me on the path to leadership. I can't thank them enough for instilling in me the core values of equity and excellence in teaching and learning. They surrounded me and my colleagues with great mentors and supporters who were doing the actual work of transforming school systems through an equity lens, and they made me believe that I could join those ranks one day. When Bob and Linda assigned me to work with Larry Leverett, I had no idea that he would serve as the beacon of excellence, integrity, and values-driven leadership for me and so many others. Larry gave me the opportunity to apply what I had learned in graduate school, and I don't know that I would have become a superintendent of schools if not for him.

The network I joined as a part of USP, and expanded throughout my career, led to the stories and examples throughout this book. So many colleagues have been incredibly generous with their time and insights into equity-based leadership that I fear naming any because I'll be sure to leave someone off the list. The same goes for the great system and school leaders that I've worked with over the years in various districts. I've learned so much from their examples.

My colleagues and board members at PDK International have been wonderfully supportive as I've been writing this book. From Rafael Heller and Teresa Preston's editing of my monthly *Kappan* column, which has made me a better writer, to Albert Chen's regular reminders that I need to stay focused and get it done, their support has enabled me to carve out the time to do the work. Frank Gitteredge, a former program officer at the W.K. Kellogg Foundation gave us a grant to support system leaders, from which I developed many of the ideas in this book, with help from former PDK Chief Program Officer Gislaine Ngounou. The Harvard Education Press team, especially Nancy Walser and Molly Grab, have provided great insight and feedback along the way, as has my good friend and colleague Meredith Honig.

Finally, every bit of any success I've had is because of the undying support of my wife Emma and my kids Eliza, Harrison, and Graham. Emma is a writer and editor and edited my dissertation back in the late 1990s. When I was a superintendent, she never failed to do her part publicly and privately to help. And her support and encouragement of me as I've sat down to write this book every morning has helped me cross the finish line.

Biography

Dr. Joshua P. Starr has been the chief executive officer of PDK International since July 2015. Since then, PDK has celebrated more than 50 years of the PDK Poll and 100 years of *Kappan* magazine. Under Dr. Starr, PDK launched Educators Rising across the nation, the first national CTE program that puts high school students on the path to becoming teachers. Educators Rising is addressing the national teacher shortage while diversifying the profession through its high school chapters, curriculum, microcredentials, and competitions. Fifty-two percent of Educators Rising participants identify as students of color. Dr. Starr has also overseen the establishment of Educators Rising Collegiate, increased foundation support for all of PDK's programs, and renewed support for PDK members and other educators. He is the author of numerous essays, book chapters, and op-eds and writes a monthly column, "On Leadership," for *Kappan*.

Prior to joining PDK, Dr. Starr was superintendent of schools in Montgomery County Public Schools in Maryland for nearly four years and previously superintendent of schools for Stamford, Connecticut, for six years. As a superintendent, Dr. Starr lead system-wide transformation efforts grounded in equity, excellence, and engagement. Dr. Starr began his career teaching Global Studies to high school special education students in Brooklyn, New York. He became a central office leader in school districts in the New York metropolitan area, including the New York City Department of Education.

Dr. Starr has a bachelor's degree in English and history from the University of Wisconsin, a master's degree in special education from Brooklyn College, and a master's and doctorate in education from the Harvard University Graduate School of Education. Dr. Starr and his wife have three children who have gone through public schools.

Index